DAVID

Other books by Larry L. Lichtenwalter:
  Well-driven Nails
  Out of the Pit: Joseph's Story and Yours
  Behind the Seen: God's Hand in Esther's Life . . . and Yours
  Wrestling With Angels

To order, call 1-800-765-6955.
  Visit us at www.reviewandherald.com for information on other Review and Herald® products.

Larry
LICHTENWALTER

A HEART LIKE HIS

REVIEW AND HERALD® PUBLISHING ASSOCIATION
HAGERSTOWN, MD 21740

The author assumes full responsibility for the accuracy of all facts and
quotations as cited in this book.

Bible texts credited to Moffatt are from: *The Bible: A New Translation,* by James
Moffatt. Copyright by James Moffatt 1954. Used by permission of Harper & Row,
Publishers, Incorporated.

Scripture quotations marked NASB are from the *New American Standard Bible,* copyright © 1960, 1962, 1963, 1968, 1971, 1972, 1973, 1975, 1977, 1974 by The
Lockman Foundation. Used by permission.

Texts credited to NIV are from the *Holy Bible, New International Version.* Copyright
© 1973, 1978, 1984, International Bible Society. Used by permission of Zondervan
Bible Publishers.

Texts credited to NKJV are from the New King James Version. Copyright © 1979,
1980, 1982 by Thomas Nelson, Inc. Used by permission. All rights reserved.

Scripture quotations marked NLT are taken from the *Holy Bible,* New Living
Translation, copyright © 1996. Used by permission of Tyndale House Publishers, Inc.,
Wheaton, Illinois 60189. All rights reserved.

Bible texts credited to NRSV are from the New Revised Standard Version of the
Bible, copyright © 1989 by the Division of Christian Education of the National Council
of the Churches of Christ in the U.S.A. Used by permission.

Bible texts credited to Phillips are from J. B. Phillips: *The New Testament in Modern
English,* Revised Edition. © J. B. Phillips 1958, 1960, 1972. Used by permission of
Macmillan Publishing Co.

This book was
Edited by Gerald Wheeler
Copyedited by Delma Miller and James Cavil
Cover designed by Leumas Design
Cover illustration by Craig Nelson/Bernstein & Andriulli, Inc.
Interior designed by Tina Ivany
Typeset: 11/14 Berkeley

PRINTED IN U.S.A.

07 06 05 04 03   5 4 3 2 1

R&H Cataloging Service
Lichtenwalter, Larry Lee, 1952-
    David—a heart like His

    1. David, king of Israel. I. Title.

                221.4092

ISBN 0-8280-1720-4

This book is dedicated to
three men of passion for God
who have touched my life profoundly:

Sal LaRosa awakened my passion for God,

Norman Dunn mentored my passion for God's work,

AND

Stuart Peters shared my passion for God
in friendship and ministry.

"Every time I think of you, I give thanks to my God"
(Phil. 1:3, NLT).

CONTENTS

Introduction: Passion and the Desert 9

1. THE LOST LIFE OF THE HEART 19
   I Samuel 16:1-13

2. THE GHOST IN THE BOTTLE 34
   I Samuel 16:13, 14

3. SOFT MUSIC FOR A HARD HEART 50
   I Samuel 16:14-23

4. LET ME OUT OF HERE! 66
   I Samuel 17:12-15

5. FRIENDLY FIRE 79
   I Samuel 17:12-30

6. IS THERE NOT A CAUSE? 89
   I Samuel 17:20-30

7. HOW TO CARRY A GIANT'S HEAD 101
   I Samuel 17:40-51, 54

8. COMMON BONDS, UNCOMMON FRIENDS 114
   I Samuel 18:1-5

9. THE SACRED ROMANCE 125
   Psalm 18:1

Epilogue: Your Strongest Instinct 135

Introduction

PASSION AND THE DESERT

D avid is one of my favorite Bible characters. I've heard or read David stories nearly all my life. I'm not sure why, but his life captures my imagination again and again. He was a youthful giant killer. Israel's most famous military commander. Son-in-law of the king. The most feared outlaw in Israel. A marauding soldier under the protection of a hostile nation. A rival Israelite king. King of all Israel. An adulterer. A murderer. A refugee king living in exile. A leader of an armed military force that killed his primary heir.[1] David's story has all the romance, mystery, intrigue, violence, love, betrayal, and majesty of the greatest epic.

I love good stories, and when I read this story my spirit soars and my heart breaks. I climb to the most noble human emotions and behavior, then plummet to the depths of my own sinful nature. I see so many things in him that I wish I had—and so many others I'm scared I do have. His story immerses me in a reality that embraces the entire range of humanness, stretching from the deep interior of my soul to the farthest reach of my imagination. Something in David's story touches my most guarded yearnings. No matter how many times I've been confronted with the biblical account of his life, I am still stirred, shocked, amazed, and forced to rethink a few hard thoughts.

David first appears in turbulent times as a nobody, someone that nobody noticed.[2] The opening words of his story ring with change: "Finally, the Lord said to Samuel, 'You have mourned long enough for Saul. I have rejected him as king of Israel. Now fill your horn with olive oil and go to Bethlehem. Find a man named Jesse who lives there, for I have selected one of his sons to be my new king'" (1 Sam. 16:1, NLT). God realizes that He has to replace Saul as king of Israel. Samuel the prophet has been grieving over Saul. Now the Lord sends Samuel to anoint a new king—an obscure young teenager who has no idea what awaits him. As the plot unfolds, David enters the story literally unnamed and dismissively referred to by his father as "the baby brother" who's out in the field watching the sheep (see verse 11). The Hebrew word Jesse used to describe his son is *haqqaton,* which carries undertones of insignificance, of not counting for very much.[3] If you are the youngest of eight brothers you're probably never going to be thought of as anything other than the kid brother (verse 11)—the family runt. Certainly no one will consider you a prime candidate for any prestigious role—especially not as king. It's a classical picture of the loneliness of a little brother accustomed to being put down, ostracized, left behind, and given the unimportant work. Because David was out of the way and mostly ignored as he watched the sheep, nobody had thought to bring him to Bethlehem that day. Yet God selected the unnamed youth whom nobody paid any attention to, and had Samuel anoint him. David was "chosen not for what anybody saw in him—not his father, his brothers, not even Samuel—but because of what God saw in him."[4]

Only at the end of this opening episode of selection and anointing does this unnoticed, uninvited, unnamed teenage shepherd—now anointed by the prophet and by the Spirit—have his name mentioned: David.[5] Thus his story begins, but by the time it ends, David has become the key figure in the life, memory, and imagination of Israel.[6] Even more so, David has become the dominant figure in the whole biblical narrative. He receives the fullest treatment of any person in Scripture. We know more about him than any other person in the Bible. Scripture presents more about David than any other biblical character. It records his name some 1,127 times—more than Abraham, Moses, Paul, and even Jesus Christ. The Bible dedicates between 54 and 66 chapters (depending on how you count)[7] to his life. And that doesn't include the 59 references to David in the New Testament or some 73 psalms accredited to his authorship.[8] No wonder David is well known in history and in modern society.[9] Christians have idealized him, children have imagined they're him, Hollywood has exploited him, artists have sculpted him, and parents have named their sons after him. Like no other individual, David captivates the imagination. His story will remain supremely fascinating as long as time remains.

When I realize how much Scripture has to say about David, I get the distinct feeling that God wants us to know this man and his life.[10] The Lord evidently feels this remarkable man has a lot to teach us. David is more than the twenty-third psalm, the killing of Goliath, and the adultery with Bathsheba. He is a man to know—a man for me to know.

One reason God wants us to know him is that, in his roles as shepherd, king, and prophet, David foreshadowed the work of his greatest descendant—Jesus Christ.[11] In many ways David prefigures Christ. As we study David, we come both to understand and appreciate our Savior in new ways. The Gospels repeatedly refer to Jesus as the "Son of David." Commenting that such a "designation isn't an incidental detail of genealogy but a major item of theology," Eugene Peterson observes that the "David story anticipates the Jesus story. The Jesus story presupposes the David story."[12] Interestingly, among the very last words spoken by Jesus in Revelation—words of hope and promise just before the curtain of the ages falls—He identifies Himself with David. "I, Jesus, have sent My angel to testify to you these things for the churches. I am the Root and the Offspring of David, the Bright and Morning Star" (Rev. 22:16, NKJV). And Revelation's celebrated Lamb, who alone is worthy to open the sealed book of divine providence and human destiny, is not only the One who is slain, but the "Root of David" (Rev. 5:5, NKJV). Jesus was the Son of David, yet in another sense He was David's ancestor. Thus Jesus of Nazareth is at once David's Lord and Son (Mark 12:35-37). As Peterson notes: "If we want to get the most out of the Jesus story, we'll want first to soak our imaginations in the David story."[13] The parallels are astonishing and illuminating.

The other reason God wants us to know this man is that David is a person with a tremendous relationship with God. The description of that relationship haunts us—Scripture calls him a man after God's own heart. David is the only recorded human that God Himself labels as having a heart like His own.[14] "The Lord has sought for Himself a man after His own heart," Samuel tells Saul when he announced how his disobedience would cost him the kingdom (1 Sam. 13:14, NKJV). The apostle Paul puts it more succinctly while preaching in Antioch: "After He [God] had re-moved him [Saul], He raised up David to be their king, concerning whom He also testified and said, 'I have found David the son of Jesse, a man after My heart, who will do all My will'" (Acts 13:22, NASB). "A man after my heart"! Awesome, isn't it? As I said, it's a haunting thought. For the life of me, I struggle with what that means. A heart like His? What is God's heart like? What about my own heart?

Evidently, David's heart was different. He had something that God saw and caused Him to say deep within Himself, "Here is someone who really connects with who I am and what I am really like." Apparently, whatever God witnessed in David's heart got to Him. One finds in Scripture an incredible commitment on God's part toward His friend David: "I have found David my servant; with my sacred oil I have anointed him. My hand will sustain him; surely my arm will strengthen him. . . . My faithful love will be with him. . . . I will maintain my love to him for-ever, and my covenant with him will never fail. I will establish his line for-ever, his throne as long as the heavens endure. . . . I will not take my love from him, nor will I ever betray my faithfulness. I will not violate my covenant or alter what my lips have uttered. Once for all, I have sworn by my holiness—and I will not lie to David" (Ps. 89:20-35, NIV). One can only wonder just what this relationship between David and God involved.

When I review David's story in search of his spiritual secret, one word comes to mind—passion. David experienced incredible victory and unpar-alleled success in his life. He was the quintessential hero—an exemplary man of faith and a magnetic leader. But it was his passion for God that stands out the most. David was an authentic man of passion with an over-whelming passion for God. As Yancey observes, "David felt more passion-ately about God than about anything else in the world, and during his reign that message trickled down to the entire nation."[15] No wonder Israel lost its heart to David more than to any other of its kings, and that it would be David alone who figures large in the nation's life, memory, and imagina-tion.[16] It was his overwhelming passion for God. That's why I keep thumb-ing back to the story of David. I know of no better model for a passionate relationship with God. That message still trickles down even after so many centuries—even to my heart. "David's strongest instinct was to relate his life to God. In comparison, nothing else mattered at all."[17] His was a God-saturated life. That's what I want. Passion. David's passion. Passion for God.

I use the word "passion"—rather than "zeal" or "enthusiasm" or "wholeheartedness"—because it speaks to the sort of inner force that David experienced and that God desires from every one of us. "I wish that you were either cold or hot," Jesus tells the lukewarm, halfhearted, passionless Laodiceans (Rev. 3:15, NRSV).

Passion is defined as "being compelled to action." Being passionate means being excited enough about a thing that you will actually do something about it. We identify passion with romance, revolution, violence, and extraordinary achievement. And we use it to explain actions that we don't understand. All we really know is that it is a force within people that drives them far beyond ordinary activities.

Mysterious in nature, passion is hard to measure and difficult to pin down. But you know when you have it, and you are quite sure when you don't. You recognize, too, when others have it. "One feels passion; it seizes you!"[18] Passion stimulates performance. People who rise to the top of business, sports, academia, science, and politics usually do so because their passion drives them. It could be a passion for power, money, notoriety, the thrill of the pursuit, or raw achievement. But whatever their motive, it calls a brand of passion into action.

Passion is a fascinating force. The ultimate time-management tool, it drives us to gain control of life. It can dull our sense of fatigue and pain and reduce or eliminate the need for pleasure or even well-being. Such passion can lead some of us to pay incredible prices to reach a desired goal. In addition, it is the energy that fuels our faith experience. Our passion for God can lift us to an extraordinary experience with God, enabling us to change things in our little worlds—our lives, our hearts, our being.[19]

As Gordon MacDonald asks: "Who of us does not crave the passion or the power to be godly people? to give witness to our faith? to serve and give selflessly? to control our drives and dispositions? But for many it is easier to talk about passion than to find it or, having found it, to maintain it."[20] Thus the haunting magnetism of David's passion for God—a passion, by the way, sustained throughout his entire life story, even while he was immersed in some of the most incredible moral failure. "David attracts attention by his vigor, his energy, his wholeheartedness, his Godheartedness."[21] In the middle of one of his psalms he shouts, "Yes, by You

I can crush a troop, and by my God I can leap over a wall!" (Ps. 18:29, paraphrase). Eugene Peterson writes how the image of David vaulting the wall catches and holds his attention. David running, coming to a stone wall, and without hesitation leaping it and continuing on his way—running toward Goliath, running from Saul, pursuing God—whatever—but always running. And leaping. Certainly not strolling or loitering.[22]

Yancey invites us to consider David, bursting with joy and cartwheeling in the streets—like an Olympic gymnast who has just won the gold medal and is out strutting his stuff—when the sacred ark symbolizing God's presence arrives with fanfare in Jerusalem. Or watch him lying prostrate on the ground for six straight nights in anguished contrition and tearfully writing a psalm of personal confession to be sung throughout the land and ultimately around the world—a psalm exposing the true nature of sin as a broken relationship with God. "Against You, You only, have I sinned," David cried out (Ps. 51:4, NKJV). As he danced before a one-Person audience, so David repented before the same audience—God.[23] And there's more.

We see David generously giving his life's accumulated wealth to build a house for God. David loving Jonathan. David angry. David pouring out the depths of his soul in imprecatory psalms or glorious praise. David showing undeserving grace to Mephibosheth. David sneaking into the sleeping camp of Saul. David attracting a band of mighty men. David hearing Goliath's blasphemies and instinctively crying out for all to hear, "Who is this uncircumcised Philistine?" David sitting before the Lord in absolute awe because of God's promise to him. And he did everything with vigor, energy, and wholeheartedness—God-heartedness. Passion!

David lived large for God for an entire lifetime. That's his secret. Passionately relating his life to God.

Do you know what you are passionate about? That's what I keep asking myself whenever I think very long about David—"What am I passionate about? And why? Am I a man of passion—with overwhelming passion for God? Do I have a heart like His?" I live in the daily awareness of how much easier it is to talk about passion than to find it or, having found it, to maintain it—let alone encourage it in others. The Bible emphasizes a relationship with a Person (rather than a doctrinal system, mystical experience, or spiritual technique), and personal relationships are never steady-state.[24] All relationships have ups and downs, what Yancey calls passion and the desert. "A relationship with an invisible God will always include uncertainty and variability,"[25] he writes. Reaching for the invisible God is no small matter. Passion is both part of that reach and its fruit. There are no shortcuts, no gimmicks, no easy ways to cultivate intimacy with God and attain the resulting passion that should carry me (or you) through life's journey.

A passion is necessary in my walk with God lest everything become "mindless or spiritless spiritual life crammed with events (not experience) and contacts (not relationships)."[26] I shudder at the thought that I would ever come to the place where I "go through the motions"—performing more out of habit than anything else. Or that my faith experience lacks energy because I have allocated it toward something other than God (the pursuit of a career, a hobby or recreational effort, or some activity that appears more daring, more pleasurable, or more personally affirming). Do God and faith and my Adventist hope still grab my imagination the way they did in my younger years when I first believed? When Jesus comes, will He find spiritual passion still burning in me? My heart resists boredom or lukewarmness. I never want to be lukewarm. How about you?

Where do we find the wellspring of passion for God? What is passion for God really like? How do you maintain such a passion, hang on to a heart like His? And what does having such a heart mean?

This volume begins a three-part journey through David's epic story in answer to these haunting questions simply because I know of no better biblical model for a passionate relationship with God than David. The king's colorful life encompasses three distinct periods that highlight his passion for God from varying perspectives—his early years, his fugitive years, and the years he reigned as Israel's king. *A Heart Like His* focuses on the initial spiritual passion of David's youthful years when God first became the absolute center of everything. *Faith on the Run* explores how the intense pressures and trials of David's fugitive years threatened to diminish his passion for God. Finally, *Dancing Like a King* tells the triumphs and fiascos of David's monarchical years (with all their leadership, family life, and ethical opportunities and dilemmas) and celebrates how he passionately lived large for God till the very end of life. This man David experienced his own passionate aspiration, "I will sing to the Lord as long as I live. I will praise my God to my last breath!" (Ps. 104:33, NLT).[27] The long march of years doesn't preclude passion. Nor need our initial passion for God ever diminish. Like David, our passion for God can radiate long and deep within—until we breathe our last or Jesus comes.

The story of David, though, is more about God than the human being. We identify easily with David—his temptations and struggles, and with the interwoven tangle of sin and obedience, success and failure, drama and boredom, that filled the days of his life. Each of us can see bits of ourselves in his life. His temptations and failures are like our own and warn us. And his courage, faithfulness, and passion for God set an example for us to follow. Yet David's story yields more than mere biblical principles about life. Its purpose is to reveal God to us—to show us what He is like and what He has done. Through this man David, God opens to us something about Himself. A heart like His? What does that tell us about God? And passion? Why is God worthy of such a thing?

---

[1] Robert D. Bergen, *1, 2 Samuel, New American Commentary* (Nashville: Broadman and Holman Publishers, 1996), vol. 7, p. 34.

[2] Walter Brueggemann, *David's Truth in Israel's Imagination and Memory* (Minneapolis: Fortress Press, 1985), p. 19; Charles R. Swindoll, *David: A Man of Passion and Destiny* (Dallas: Word Publishing, 1997), pp. 13-25.

[3] On the Hebrew word for "youngest," cf. L. J. Copples, קָטָן (*qātān*)—"Young, insignificant, little"—in *Theological Wordbook of the Old Testament,* vol. 2, pp. 795-797.

[4] Eugene Peterson, *Leap Over a Wall: Earthly Spirituality for Everyday Christians* (New York: HarperSanFrancisco, 1997), p. 17.

[5] *Ibid.,* p. 24.

[6] Brueggemann, p. 19.

[7] See Swindoll, p. 4; Keith Kaynor, *When God Chooses: The Life of David* (Schaumburg, Ill.: Regular Baptist Press, 1989), p. 8.

[8] Theodore H. Epp, *A Man After the Heart of God* (Lincoln, Nebr.: Back to the Bible Broadcast, 1965), p. 212.

[9] Several recent scholarly books and articles—while calling into question details about the life rule of David and debating whether or not he was a hero or a scoundrel—are affirming that David is clearly a historical figure. See Jeffery Sheler, "King David: Not the Man He Used to Be?" *U.S. News and World Report,* Mar. 19, 2001, p. 45.

[10] Kaynor, p. 9. The New Testament Jesus likewise depicts Jesus as a shepherd (John 10:1-18; 1 Peter 5:4), a king (John 18:37; 19:21), and a prophet (Luke 1:76; 4:24; 13:33; 24:19; Acts 3:22). Since David, the first member of Israel's royal Messianic line, functioned in these three roles, it seems appropriate that Jesus the Messiah should be depicted by the New Testament writers not only as inheriting these roles but as superseding David's accomplishments in them.

[11] Bergen, p. 465.

[12] Peterson, p. 9.

[13] *Ibid.*

[14] Without doubt, many others had a tremendous relationship with God. I can think of

Enoch, Joseph, and Daniel. And there's John, the disciple whom Jesus loved. But David's story is the fullest and most extended human story God gives us. David alone receives that designation.

[15] Philip Yancey, *Reaching for the Invisible God* (Grand Rapids: Zondervan Publishing House, 2000), p. 190.

[16] Frederick Buechner, *Peculiar Treasures: A Biblical Who's Who* (New York: Harper & Row, Publishers, 1979), p. 24.

[17] Yancey, p. 192.

[18] Gordon MacDonald, *Restoring Your Spiritual Passion* (Nashville: Oliver-Nelson, 1986), p. 14.

[19] See MacDonald, pp. 10-23; and Marcia Wieder, *Doing Less and Having More: Five Easy Steps for Discovering What You Really Want—And Getting It* (New York: William Morrow and Company, Inc., 1998), pp. 97-99.

[20] MacDonald, p. 10.

[21] Peterson, p. 11.

[22] *Ibid.*

[23] Yancey, pp. 190-192.

[24] *Ibid.*, p. 188.

[25] *Ibid.*

[26] MacDonald, p. 8.

[27] While Psalm 104 names no author, it exhibits many indications of David's touch, and the Septuagint claims it for David (see F. B. Meyer, *Gems From the Psalms* [Westchester, Ill.: Good News Publishers, 1976], p. 168; and Derek Kidner, *Psalms 73-150* [Downers Grove, Ill.: Inter-Varsity Press, 1975], p. 367). Because of its common framework and style—its exordium and conclusion, calling on the singer's "soul" or "whole being," to bless the Lord—commentators often pair Psalm 104 (as companion psalms) with Psalm 103, which clearly identifies itself as a psalm of David. While their themes are different, both Psalm 103 and Psalm 104 begin with an individual self-exhortation to praise, then develop into a communal hymn of praise, and conclude with a reiteration of its preliminary self-exhortation. Their common framework must have provided the reason for their pairing right at the beginning of a collection of songs of praise, Psalms 103-107. In Psalm 63:4 David utters similar sentiments: "I will bless You as long as I live" (NASB).

THE LOST LIFE OF THE HEART

I Samuel 16:1-13

When she was only 25 Holly Lagalante shelled out $2,500 for an eyelid lift. The tab nearly maxed out her credit card, but the results—more bright-eyed, less droopy—left her absolutely giddy. Two years later Lagalante, a petite blond from suburban Chicago, was back for liposuction on her thighs. "I'd love to have Heather Locklear's body," she says. Then came varicose-vein removal. And, later, a forehead peel. Holly had $7,000 left to pay off when she lost her $9-an-hour job managing a health-food store, moved in with her mother, and filed for bankruptcy. Still, she claimed she was happier and more self-confident since her body overhaul and had no regrets. When Holly landed a new job as a salesclerk at a local mall, she declared that when she finished paying off her debt she'd reward herself—with a forehead lift or maybe liposuction to fix her saggy knees. "It's been tough on me financially, but it's worth every penny," she says. "It's life-changing." [1]

Not so long ago, aspiring starlets and women "of a certain age" were pretty much the only patients who went under the knife for cosmetic surgery—and they did so in secret. But now the image-conscious of all ages—and genders—are seeking the perfect body. The cosmetic craze includes laser skin resurfacing, fat injection or liposuction, nose reshaping, breast augmentation, eyelid surgery, thigh lift, buttock lift, tummy tuck, upper arm lift, forehead lift, cheek implants, scalp reduction, ear reshaping, antiwrinkle injection, calf implants, pectoral implants, and chin augmentation. You can have it all if you got the bucks.

We live in a world obsessed with externals. Visit any health club. Wall-to-wall mirrors reflect people looking at themselves as they pump iron. Stop for a moment and study them watching themselves. Check out the stylish Oscars or Emmy Awards crowd, the ritzy country music scene, or fashionable Miss America pageant. Observe the tattoos and body piercing. Notice the ads on television—from cosmetics to clothing to perfume to razors and soaps and hair creams. Most have a single message: Make yourself look better, more attractive, more beautiful. Be sexy, muscular, youthful . . . or downright unique! Image is today's marketing norm. This focus on externals does not involve just physical appearance. It includes one's abilities and what they've achieved or acquired—a Ph.D., money, power, some status position, that well-located swank home, or fancy car, gadgets, etc. Everything is just as the Lord whispered into Samuel's ear: "Man looks at the outward appearance" (1 Sam. 16:7, NKJV).

Surprisingly, the prophet Samuel too at first focused on externals. After arguing with God about the personal dangers inherent in anointing another king behind Saul's back, Samuel dutifully filled his horn with oil and set out with a cover story[2] for the Bethlehem home of a man named Jesse. When he arrived in Bethlehem the town elders trembled in fear. Pastors (especially prophets) don't usually show up out of the blue for no reason. Samuel, though, announced his peaceful intentions and invited the village to attend a special sacrifice to the Lord.

When Jesse arrived at the festivities with seven sons, the prophet's heart leaped at the sight. He should have known better, but the moment Eliab, Jesse's eldest, entered the room, the prophet thought to himself, *"Surely the Lord's anointed is before Him"* (verse 6, NKJV). Eliab, we're told, had a princely bearing and more nearly resembled Saul in stature and handsomeness than the others.[3] He was certainly kingly material. But Samuel was about to learn a very important lesson: "Do not look at his appearance or at the height of his stature," the Lord whispered, "because I have rejected him; for God sees not as man sees, for man looks at the outward appearance, but the Lord looks at the heart" (verse 7, NASB). God reminded Samuel that the human mind has an overwhelming tendency to make assumptions based on appearances. The Lord, however, probes to the heart. Here we have one of the most profound statements in all of Scripture regarding divine concerns and human capacities. The Lord has the distinct ability to observe and judge a person's heart—their thoughts, emotions, attitudes, and intentions. The secret things. Everything. On God's scales heart matters outweigh all other aspects of human life.[4]

This opening episode plays on the Hebrew verb "see," purposefully contrasting what human beings notice with what God perceives (verses 1, 6, 7). Human beings restrict themselves to mere outward forms, while God examines the heart. The biblical contrast does not mean that externals are entirely irrelevant or inherently evil. I am glad my wife takes care how she looks. But looks can be deceiving and the exterior just that—a veneer, window dressing for a barren or hurting heart.

While holding meetings in Odessa, Ukraine, I had a woman come to me with her troubled teenage granddaughter. The only committed Christian in her home, the grandmother hoped that I could lead her granddaughter to Christ. Netanya had been attending church with grandma for some time and had been coming to my evangelistic meetings. But she was resisting and resenting most of what she was hearing. Beyond that, though—and what troubled grandma most—her behavior and moods expressed some obvious emotional turmoil in her life. As I met with Netanya that afternoon, she told me she'd never become a Christian. "Why wouldn't you open your life to Jesus?" I asked. "Why do you feel the way you do about what it means to follow Him?" Her answers revolved mainly around "do's and don'ts"—the externals, especially jewelry, cosmetics, and clothing. Netanya wasn't convinced that these exterior things were all that important. "It's what's inside!" I remember her saying again and again. I hadn't brought any of these subjects up in my presentations. Evidently, grandma had.

I readily agreed with Netanya that it's what's inside that really counts with God. The Lord looks on the heart. What's in the heart matters more than what's on the finger or on one's face. I told her, too, that the heart priority can be a wonderfully freeing truth. But when I pressed her as to why these externals should be such a big problem for her, she finally opened a crack to her hurting heart. Netanya confided that she didn't feel very pretty inside. She believed that her clothes and cosmetics and jewelry simply made her feel better about herself. Interestingly, she had been telling me that externals were not important because it's what's inside that counts, yet inside she was painfully empty, feeling ugly, and those unimportant externals were the only thing she could think of that could make her feel pretty inside. My heart cried.

I saw Netanya a few years later, now an extraordinarily beautiful young woman—dressed to kill, complete with blond hair, cosmetics, jewelry, fancy clothes, and . . . still feeling not very pretty inside. To focus on externals is to overlook the real criteria for determining what a person is actually like and what's really going on inside. We have an overwhelming tendency to make assumptions based on appearances—even about ourselves. But according to God, only what's inside really counts.

Claiming It All

But what is this thing we call the heart? What is it that God is so intent on exploring? In Scripture the word "heart" refers to the center of an individual's mental, emotional, moral, and spiritual life. It's our innermost being, our internal private world—who we really are deep down inside.[5] As our *mental center,* the heart knows, understands, reflects, considers, and remembers. Serving as our *emotional center,* it is the seat of joy, courage, pain, anxiety, despair, sorrow, and fear. Then as our *moral center,* it orients us in terms of our values and choices between right and wrong and good and bad. And, finally, as our *spiritual center,* the heart connects us with spiritual/moral realities beyond our human experience.[6]

In their book *The Sacred Romance* coauthors Brent Curtis and John Eldredge help us catch a more down-to-earth glimpse into what we're talking about: "The life of the heart is a place of great mystery. Yet we have many expressions to help us express this flame of the human soul. We describe a person without compassion as 'heartless,' and we urge him or her to 'have a heart.' Our deepest hurts we call 'heartaches.' Jilted lovers are 'brokenhearted.' Courageous soldiers are 'bravehearted.' The truly evil are 'black-hearted' and saints have 'hearts of gold.' If we need to speak at the most intimate level, we ask for a 'heart-to-heart' talk. 'Lighthearted' is how we feel on vacation. And when we love someone as truly as we may, we love 'with all our heart.' But when we lose our passion for life, when a deadness sets in which we cannot seem to shake, we confess, 'My heart's just not in it.'

"In the end, it doesn't matter how well we have performed or what we have accomplished—a life without heart is not worth living. For out of this wellspring of our soul flows all true caring and all meaningful work, all real worship and all sacrifice. Our faith, hope, and love issue from this fount, as well. Because it is in our heart that we first hear the voice of God and it is in the heart that we come to know Him and learn to live in His love."[7]

Furthermore, each of us has two stories. "On the outside, there is the external story of our lives. This is the life everyone sees, our life of work and play and church, of family and friends, paying bills, and growing older. Our external story is where we carve out the identity most others know."[8] "The inner life, the story of our heart, is the life of the deep places within us, our passions and dreams, our fears and our deepest wounds. It is the unseen life, the mystery within."[9] "The true story of every person in this world is not the story you see, the external story. The true story of each person is the journey of his or her heart."[10] This story of our heart is what God is interested in. The heart is where we both genuinely experience and express our passion for Him.

Curtis and Eldredge further assert that if we live only in the outer story, eventually we will lose track of our inner life. When we move our spiritual life into the outer world of activity or physical appearance or other externals, we drift internally. We cannot hear the voice of God if we have lost touch with our heart. Thus, to lose heart is to lose everything. To focus on externals is to go out of focus. This is why God tells us, "Above all else, guard your heart, for it is the wellspring of life" (Prov. 4:23, NIV). God knows that to lose heart is to lose everything—especially Him. Jesus pressed it further, deeper: "Love the Lord your God with all your heart and with all your soul and with all your strength and with all your mind" (Luke 10:27, NIV). Not just a little bit, but all of it. The heart is what passion is all about, from where it must spring, and how much it must claim.

Our heart, then, is the key to passion for God. It should come as no surprise that "the heart does not respond to principles and programs; it seeks not efficiency, but passion. Art, poetry, beauty, mystery, ecstasy.

These are what rouse the heart. Indeed, they are the language that must be spoken if one wishes to communicate with the heart."[11] Passion is impossible without the heart. It is what the heart seeks. Furthermore, passion cannot exist without involving the "whole" heart. For passion to be passion it must claim it all. It's all or nothing! Only when passion claims the whole heart can we say that it has truly seized us rather than our trying to create it.

So What Did God See?

Samuel dutifully went down Jesse's list, and with each son who passed by, God said, "Nope! This is not the one!" Seven sons, seven no's! By now the prophet was puzzled. He could see only externals. These were Jesse's sons. Had he missed something? Did he misunderstand God's instructions? Was he losing his prophetic edge? Did he have the right town? "This *is* Bethlehem, isn't it?" Did he have the right family? "You *are* Jesse, aren't you?" Well—there must be another son. "Are these all the sons you have?" Samuel finally asked (1 Sam. 16:11, NLT).

"'There is still the youngest,' Jesse replied. 'But he's out in the fields watching the sheep'" (verse 11, NLT).

"Send for him right now," Samuel commanded. "We're not going to sit down to eat until he's here" (see verse 11).

David arrived on the scene with no idea what awaited him. He didn't look much different from any of the other Jewish boys his age. Scripture simply records that "he was ruddy, with beautiful eyes and a handsome appearance" (verse 12, NASB). That's the only physical description we have of David. He was handsome, had beautiful eyes, and had a reddish complexion[12] (and no doubt smelled like sheep). As Samuel gazed on this handsome young man, he waited. He had already made a mistake based on appearances. Then God whispered, "Rise and anoint him; he is the one" (verse 12, NIV).

I can't help wondering what the prophet must have been thinking while anointing David—*What's in this guy's heart that God sees and so favors?* It's a good question. When God looked beyond David's outward appearance and deep within his heart, what did He find? According to Scripture, one can have an "evil heart" (Gen. 6:5; Ps. 101:4; Prov. 6:18;

24

Heb. 3:12), be "godless in heart" (Job 36:13), or be "perverse and deceitful in heart" (Prov. 11:20; Jer. 17:9). A person may "harden his heart" (Deut. 15:7; Ps. 95.8; Heb. 3:8, 15; 4:7). But an individual can also have a "clean heart" (Ps. 51:10; Heb. 10:22), an "upright heart" (Ps. 7:10; 11:2; 32:11; 94:15), a "pure heart" (Ps. 24:4), and can receive a "new heart" (Eze. 18:31; 36:26). What about David? The psalms he authored give us a rich source in which to answer this question.[13] They convey his view of God and the passion of his heart, because they arose out of David's life experiences and God's dealings with him.[14] When we place his psalms alongside the historical details of his story—which report his actions, behavior, words, choices, and descriptions of his attitudes and moods—they reveal the habits of his heart. They portray how his heart characteristically turned. In his psalms we not only catch a glimpse of David's view of God, we also find glimpses of his inner self.

F. B. Meyer observes that many of the psalms that can be attributed to his youthful years reflect his heart "because they are so free from the pressure of sorrow and anxiety."[15] Psalms 8, 19, 23, and 29 reveal a sense of wonder that God should pay attention to humanity at all, yet are full of confidence that He was David's shepherd. Deeply stirred by the awesomeness of the heavens, he also was convinced that the words of God were equally divine. These psalms show him afraid of what might be secret faults and presumptuous sins. While David longed to join the chorus of praise he heard in the orchestra of nature, "he was certain that there were yearnings and faculties within his soul that nature could not participate in and that made him nature's high priest and chorister."[16]

As we read through his psalms we learn that David had a *believing heart.* "The fool has said in his heart, 'There is no God,'" he writes (Ps. 14:1, NKJV; 53:1, NKJV). You cannot have passion if you don't believe firmly in something. And there can be no passion for God without belief in His existence. As Scripture makes it clear, "without faith it is impossible to please God, because anyone who comes to him must believe that he exists and that he rewards those who earnestly seek him" (Heb. 11:6, NIV). The kind of intense search referred to here implies a brand of passion. Such passion leaves no room for double-mindedness. If passion is to claim it all—all the heart and soul and strength and mind—there must be wholehearted belief. "With the heart one believes," Paul asserts (Rom.

10:10, NKJV). When God looked at David's heart He saw a young man who firmly believed in His existence. Such a passion for God could claim David's whole heart because he believed with his whole heart. It's as Oswald Chambers says: "It is by the heart that God is perceived [known] and not by reason . . . so that is what faith is: God perceived by the heart." When you really believe in something, passion will always claim your heart. All of it!

David also had a *thirsty heart.* "O God, you are my God, earnestly I seek you; my soul thirsts for you, my body longs for you, in a dry and weary land where there is no water" (Ps. 63:1, NIV). "As the deer pants for streams of water, so my soul pants for you, O God. My soul thirsts for God, for the living God. When can I go and meet with God?" (Ps. 42:1, 2, NIV).[17] Desire is an incredible component of passion. Without desire, there can be no passion. Such desire implies a sense of need or want, a yearning for something more, something you don't have within yourself. It creates a constant restlessness. Passion spontaneously overflows from a heart that yearns for something that it senses will meet its need. David's thirst points toward such a heartfelt desire. He has an intense need of God. As a thirsty deer in a barren wilderness longs for a cool stream, David literally pants for God. Deeply restless and unsatisfied without God, he thirsts for God because the Lord has become so incredibly real to Him that in his heart he feels life itself would no longer be either real or complete without Him. David's strongest instinct was to relate his life to God. In comparison, nothing else mattered. As A. W. Tozer suggests: "Thirsty hearts are those whose longings have been wakened by the touch of God within them." Such a longing had indeed awakened in David, and passion for God naturally followed. Passion could claim it all because there was genuine thirst. "When can I go and meet with God?"

Finally, David had an *open heart.* "Examine me, O Lord, and try me; test my mind and my heart," he writes (Ps. 26:2, NASB). "Search me, O God, and know my heart; try me and know my anxious thoughts; and see if there be any hurtful way in me, and lead me in the everlasting way" (Ps. 139:23, 24, NASB). These are intensely personal thoughts. David keenly recognizes God's capacity to explore the human heart. "O Lord, you have searched me and you know me. You know when I sit and when I rise; you perceive my thoughts from afar. You discern my going out and my lying down; you are familiar with all my ways. Before a word is on my tongue you know it completely, O Lord. You hem me in—behind and before; you have laid your hand upon me. Such knowledge is too wonderful for me, too lofty for me to attain" (verses 1-6, NIV). Not only does God see the invisible and penetrates the inaccessible; His knowledge of us is personal and active: "You have searched me!" David senses diligent, difficult, and personal probing. God is exploring, digging into, and examining him through and through as He searches for telling facts and information for building a picture of David's character. God is completely familiar with his most common and casual moments. Even his thoughts are an open book. In fact, God monitors the whole process of his thought-life. He sees and understands what goes on. The Lord knows what makes him tick, why he is who he is and does what he does.

"This blows my mind," David cries (see verse 6). It's hard to believe. In fact, it's scary. We have an instinctive urge to want to avoid God's face, to escape from Him. "Where can I go from your Spirit? Where can I flee from your presence? If I go up to the heavens, you are there; if I make my bed in the depths, you are there. If I rise on the wings of the dawn, if I settle on the far side of the sea, even there your hand will guide me, your right hand will hold me fast. If I say, 'Surely the darkness will hide me and the light become night around me,' even the darkness will not be dark to you; the night will shine like the day, for darkness is as light to you" (verses 7-12, NIV).

The things God knew about him could have made David nervous, yet he prays, "Search me, O God, and know my heart; try me and know my anxious thoughts; and see if there be any hurtful way in me, and lead me in the everlasting way" (verses 23, 24, NASB). David wants to be God's man at any cost, so he unveils his inner being—purposefully, consciously, right down to where unspoken thoughts dwell and unstated motives hide out in secret. He invites God's searchlight to bathe him. Then David goes even further. He asks the Lord to find out which thoughts or tendencies lead him away from fellowship with God. "Show them to me so I can understand them and their effect on my walk with You," he says. That's passion! Authentic passion can seize only open, transparent hearts. If we're self-protective or nervous about the things taking place deep within us, we'll never abandon ourselves to anything, let alone God. Nor will passion ever fuel us if we're reserved, holding ourselves back in any way. It's an all-or-none kind of thing. The kind of intimacy and openness this psalm implies generates passion—a desire to be real, and close. It's a fundamental fact of life: no openness, no intimacy, no passion. When we refuse to allow God to get close enough to really know what we're like (even though He already does), we'll never get close enough to Him to find out what He's really like.

Still Searching

David's uniqueness becomes clear when we remember that none of his seven brothers qualified in God's eyes. The number seven represents a large number, suggesting that even among so many the Lord did not find the one He was looking for.[18] Scripture tells us that "the eyes of the Lord move to and fro throughout the earth that He may strongly support those whose heart is completely His" (2 Chron. 16:9, NASB). God's eyes are everywhere, always searching, still searching today, for those who are so wholehearted in their relationship with Him that through them He might reveal His great power and perform His wondrous works. He still tests the mind and the heart (Jer. 17:10; 20:12). None of us know the day or hour when God will pass by, seeking for a heart like His, searching for men and women who love Him with all their heart and all their soul and all their strength and all their mind. God yearns for hearts inflamed with such undivided passion for Him. When we least expect it, we are being scrutinized, watched, and tested in the daily commonplaces to see whether we have the right stuff. It's passion God seeks, because passion claims it all.

When God looked through the land in search of a new king for Israel, He found only one with the kind of passion He needed—David. Only David had a heart like His—the kind of heart whose strongest instinct was to relate its life to Him. And only David had the kind of passion for God that would claim his entire heart. That's because David early nurtured the heart qualities that would awaken and sustain passion for God. David had a believing heart, a thirsting heart, and an open heart. Passion can never claim our heart for God if we don't really believe in Him. Nor can passion ever propel our heart toward God if we have no sense of our need of Him. And finally, passion for God can never exist in us without the kind of intimacy an openness to Him implies. If passion is to claim it all (our all), we must believe in God, sense our need of Him, and unveil ourselves before Him.

What about you? What is your heart like? What is your passion quotient? How would you answer the urgent questions David's story raises about your heart? I must also look into my own life. Do I have a believing heart? Do I have a thirsting heart? Do I have an open heart? Has passion for God claimed my all? When God looks beyond my external appearance, what does He see?

The heart is the key to passion for God. Passion is impossible without it—all of it. Every one of us experiences the incessant duality of human nature—the fickleness of our hearts. We all discover in ourselves elements of that man or that woman who is after God's heart, and also another man, another woman who is most unlike God's heart. As fallen human beings we both believe in Him and doubt Him at the same time. Although we thirst for Him, we then satiate ourselves with other things. Thus we open ourselves to Him, only to draw back lest He get too close. And while we desire passion for God, we are afraid of what both He and this passion will do to us. "Love the Lord your God with all your heart and with all your soul and with all your strength and with all your mind" (Luke 10:27, NIV). It sounds like the right thing, but . . . it takes passion. Passion we're not sure we have the energy for. It's easier to be lukewarm, halfhearted, passionless.

The ministry of Sal LaRosa awakened my passion for God. I was in the fifth grade, my first year in church school. My dad often reminds me that none of the parents in my neighborhood wanted their children to play with me, because—well, my language, my dirty mind, my aggressiveness. Accompanying him to the barrooms and watching him earn money at pool, I drank his beer and sneaked his cigarettes. I was going to be like him in every way—tough, cocky, assertive, and self-contained. Somewhere along the way Dad told my mom that she could take my three sisters and create Adventists out of them, but he'd make me like him. That was fine with me. I had found Christianity dull and boring. It wasn't for men (or boys). Besides, I had allocated my energies to other more tangible and gratifying pursuits.

Fifth-grade math was boring, to say the least. It was more than I had a mind to deal with. And I jumped at the chance to get out of it. One day my teacher announced that Pastor LaRosa was going to begin a Bible study class—and it would meet during math time. Sounded good to me. And so began my journey with God as I skipped math to hang out with this outgoing pastor and take his Bible lessons—never dreaming where it would lead. I don't remember any of the studies or even how many there were. But somewhere along the way God touched my heart, and something mysterious awakened deep inside. I didn't realize it at first. And I didn't quite understand it when I did.

My inner journey through the next few months was a roller coaster. Torn between two lovers, as one song goes, I acted the fool, struggling to believe, but thinking it all a joke. I thirsted for God as I had never thought I would or could, yet I also earnestly longed to keep everything my dad's world had to offer. And while I wanted to open my heart to this unseen God, I was scared to death at how concretely personal and life-changing that exercise might be. But for some reason I kept at it. Maybe I should say, God graciously kept at it. He persisted with this mysterious awakening. The more I lingered at His visitations, the more I thirsted. Just as Tozer says: "Thirsty hearts are those whose longings have been wakened by the touch of God within them." It was happening to me.

Most of it is a blur after so many years, but I remember the turmoil of letting go. The struggle. The tears. The apprehension. The heartbreaking choice—between my dad's world and life with God. At the time I saw no possible middle ground. To choose God meant some sort of break with Dad—whom I loved and idolized. But to go with Dad would somehow cost me this unexplainable experience with God. Somewhere along the way I gave in and reached for this invisible God with all my heart. It was the most glorious moment of my life. I am what I am today because of that awakening and reaching out. Although I still can't see God, the passion for Him that that experience engendered has never left my heart. No matter my ups and downs through the years, it still burns.

In the middle of it all was Pastor LaRosa. Outgoing. Personal. Animated. Fun to be around. A captivating speaker, he was a military veteran and a muscular gymnast. And deeply spiritual. He knew God. In fact, he talked about God as if He were absolutely real and the only thing worth living for. His unblushing passion for the Lord gripped my imagination and beckoned my heart. Here was a "real man" in touch with God, something for a boy who wanted to be a "man" to really think about. LaRosa was a male role model contrasting sharply with my father. That mentoring was providential, I believe. Especially the passion—passion that showed in his prayers, his preaching, his personal invitations to my heart. Passion that animated all his talk about God and his telling me how the gospel ministry was a worthy calling. It was here with him, during my early teen years, that both my passion for God awakened and my vision for ministry took root.

Years later I was speaking to some pastors at a conference workers' retreat and had the unexpected surprise of meeting LaRosa again after not seeing him for nearly a quarter century. It was a moving moment for both of us. As we sat and talked at length about God and His leading in our lives, we both confided our apprehensions. I first wondered what it would be like to see him again after so many years. Would the same chemistry be there? Had he changed? Would he still have the passion? Had years of ministry or his life experiences or his retirement jaded his ardor for God in any way? What about his attitudes toward the church and ministry? Would he really be all that interested in what God had been doing in my life? Would he be proud of me? Was it OK for me to want him to be proud of me? Would we touch again at the coals of a common fire for God? I realized that after so long, he was still a mentor in my imagination.

LaRosa himself wondered whether I'd really notice him. No longer youthful, he was retired now and out of the action, with hair as white as snow. I was pastoring a big church, had a Ph.D., authored books, taught at the seminary, and become a sought-after speaker for all kinds of events. More than he'd ever done or been, so he thought. Why would I spend time with him? What would there be to talk about, except the usual niceties about family and how we were doing and listing our achievements or the places we'd pastored? Would we go deep, or be superficial in our sharing? Would we really connect again on that all-important matter—God and our passion for Him?

What would our surprise reunion bring? We both wondered.

The fact that we both confided our apprehensions at meeting after so many years—and the kind of questions that haunted our hearts—lets you know the answer to most of our existential musings and the level on which we quickly connected. After all those years we identified again on that all-important matter—God and our passion for Him. For me, it was an existential moment that pulled me back to my spiritual roots—of who I am today and why. It reminded me, too, of what I ever want to be—passionate for God. After having seen so many who have lost their passion through the years (or never quite really found it), encountering LaRosa's still-burning fire was a welcome blessing.

A few weeks later I received a note from this man of passion for God: "Larry, when we met after so long a time, let me tell you, the blessing traveled in both directions. How wonderful to see you, talk with you, and reminisce. Nothing has changed with you except growth and advancement in the Lord. You are the same Larry—warm, spiritual, outgoing, and unaffected by your success. Praise God!"

I cried when I read those words. They still stir me. Because I don't want anything to change in me since that first awakening except growth and advancement in the Lord. I want to be the same Larry—so filled with passion that God has claimed my whole heart. I never want passion for God to leave my heart. No matter what life brings, I want it to "still burn." I want to reach for God until there is no more breath in me. Till Jesus comes.

Thus the power of David's story. Nowhere else is there such a dramatic example of passion that, once awakened, never dissipates. Why? Because passion claimed it all.

---

[1] Claudia Kalb, "Our Quest to Be Perfect," *Newsweek,* Aug. 9, 1999, p. 52.

[2] Understanding Samuel's uneasiness, God provided a spiritual context in which he could carry out His purposes without being discovered. The prophet was to take a heifer to Bethlehem and offer a sacrifice to the Lord. This sincere worship experience also became a divine method of protecting Samuel from Saul.

[3] Ellen G. White, *Patriarchs and Prophets* (Mountain View, Calif.: Pacific Press Pub. Assn., 1958), p. 638.

[4] "No outward beauty can recommend the soul to God. The wisdom and excellence revealed in the character and deportment, express the true beauty of the man; and it is the inner worth, the excellency of the heart, that determines our acceptance with the Lord of hosts" (*Ibid.*).

[5] On the Hebrew word for "heart," cf. A. Bowling, לֵבָב (*lēbāb*)—"Heart, understanding, mind" in *Theological Wordbook of the Old Testament,* vol. 1, pp. 466, 467.

[6] Adapted from Gene A. Getz, *David: Seeking God Faithfully* (Nashville: Broadman and Holman Publishers, 1995), pp. 18, 19.

[7] Brent Curtis and John Eldredge, *The Sacred Romance: Drawing Closer to the Heart of God* (Nashville: Thomas Nelson Publishers, 1997), p. 3.

[8] *Ibid.,* p. 5.

[9] *Ibid.,* p. 6.

[10] *Ibid.,* p. 7.

[11] *Ibid.,* p. 6.

[12] He may have had red hair or, more likely, he was reddened or bronzed from the hours he spent out in the sun and the wind.

[13] The book of Psalms divides into four basic collections: the Davidic Psalms, Psalms of Asaph, Psalms of the Sons of Korah, and the Songs of Ascents. These four collections further fall into five "books": Book I (Ps. 1-41); Book II (Ps. 42-72); Book III (Ps. 73-89); Book IV (Ps. 90-106); and Book V (Ps. 107-150). The Davidic Psalms include several selections: Psalms 3-41 (with the possible exception of Psalm 33); Psalms 51-70 (with the possible exceptions of Psalms 66 and 67); and Psalms 138-145. These three collections do not constitute all of David's psalms, of which there are 73. Others may have formed smaller collections (Psalms 108-110), while yet others, which now stand alone, may have belonged to collections initially, but were moved to another position in the Psalms by the editors for some theological or liturgical reason. In the process some psalms may have lost their clear Davidic link (Ps. 42; 104, etc.). Several psalms express an obvious Davidic thought, touch, and feel, but are anonymous, likely having been absorbed into one of the other basic collections (Asaph, Korah, Ascents). See Peter C. Craigie, *Psalms 1-50, Word Biblical Commentary* (Waco, Tex.: Word Books, 1983), vol. 19, pp. 28-31.

[14] Theodore H. Epp, *A Man After the Heart of God,* p. 212.

[15] F. B. Meyer, *The Life of David: The Man After God's Own Heart* (Lynnwood, Wash.: Emerald Books, 1996), p. 14.

[16] *Ibid.*

[17] While the expression and setting of Psalm 42 may be the sons of Korah (2 Chron. 20:19), the thoughts are evidently David's, perhaps written while he was in exile from Absalom. See F. B. Meyer, *Gems From the Psalms,* p. 68. Ellen White hints that David composed it while he was "a hunted fugitive, finding refuge in the rocks and caves of the wilderness" (Ellen G. White, *Education* [Mountain View, Calif.: Pacific Press Pub. Assn., 1952], p. 164).

[18] Ralph W. Klein, *1 Samuel, Word Biblical Commentary* (Waco, Tex.: Word Books, 1983), vol. 10, pp. 161, 162.

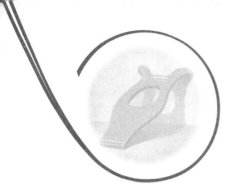

2

THE GHOST IN THE BOTTLE

I Samuel 16:13, 14

The allure of fragrance is real. So much so that the perfume industry has become a $15 billion-a-year business creating a commodity no one really needs but almost everyone wants. Perfumers incessantly search for a fragrance so wonderful that it completely entrances us. A perfume so beautiful that men will miss a woman when she leaves the room. A scent so haunting that it beguiles us into believing our innermost dreams will come true. Perfume can be wondrously evocative. It is more than just a whiff of costly air. Because the sense of smell plugs smack into our brain's limbic system—the seat of emotion (no other sense has such immediate access)—perfume can erase bad memories, trigger pleasant ones, make us feel good, or stir up dreams. We crave to be prettier, richer, sexier, happier than we are. So perfumers sell hope. "Perfume is a promise in a bottle," they say.[1] Consider the names on the labels of the fragrances we buy: Joy, Pleasures, White Diamonds, Opium, Beautiful, Allure.

Finding the right essence can be downright confusing. Whenever I step into one of those large department stores the myriad of fragrances emanating from the strategically positioned Perfume Department literally energizes my senses. As I pass by it to whatever other department I'm on my way to, I often catch a haunting whiff of something that really speaks to me. Usually when I stop to explore which one it is, though, I can never find it. After a few moments of searching, my olfactory sense overloads and distinct fragrances blur. It's frustrating!

One Christmas I wanted to get just the right fragrance for my wife, Kathie. It had to be something that was both silky soft and unforgettably evocative. The kind of fragrance that invades your space with a gentle loveliness and haunts your imagination with delight. I wanted something that, when I smelled it, instantly made me think of her. After several occasions of sniffing around the perfume counters and taking home samples sprayed on cards, I finally stumbled upon Christian Dior's Dolce Vita (Beautiful Life). M-m-m-m. Do I ever enjoy that fragrance! So does Kathie. When she daubs a bit of Dolce Vita body creme on her wrists and behind her ears as an aromatic base to the more potent perfumed oil, I can smell her several rooms away. Often on a Sabbath morning I'm down in my office rehearsing my sermon, and this fragrance wafts through the air ducts. I know she's up. It makes me think of her. Memory, fragrance, imagination, feelings—all intertwining. Dolce Vita.

I have one problem, though. Other women wear Dolce Vita too. When I catch a whiff of it I instinctively turn and . . . well, it's not my wife. In the end, there's more to it than just the "scent of a woman."

Invasive Symbol

The oil Samuel used to anoint David with exuded an evocative and memorable fragrance. I can picture that intimate and private moment. The aging white-haired prophet and the youthful, bronzed shepherd with the beautiful eyes. Samuel hears the Spirit whisper in his ears: "Arise, anoint him; for this is he." Then he takes the horn of oil and anoints David. Samuel had not revealed his errand even to the family of Jesse,[2] and he performed the anointing ceremony in secret.[3] Evidently Samuel and David quietly met somewhere alone. Or perhaps his brothers were so distracted with the festivities that they didn't notice what was going on. Whatever, Samuel popped the cork in the horn of oil that he had brought with him from Nob and lavishly poured the fragrant substance over David's head. As the oil drips down his hair, flows down his neck, and trickles down the full length of his body, I can picture Samuel's trembling hand pushing back the clustering locks of David's hair and his lips whispering softly into the astonished lad's ear the thrilling meaning of the symbol: "You will be the next king."[4]

Samuel didn't employ just any-old-everyday cooking oil to anoint David. He used exclusive "holy oil." Not the kind you would find at the local market, but perfumed oil reserved only for sacred things and for anointing priests and kings. God says, "I have found David My servant; with My holy oil I have anointed him" (Ps. 89:20, NASB). The exclusive formula for this specialty oil can be found in Exodus. "Moreover, the Lord spoke to Moses, saying, 'Take also for yourself the finest of spices: of flowing myrrh five hundred shekels, and of fragrant cinnamon half as much, two hundred and fifty, and of fragrant cane two hundred and fifty, and of cassia five hundred, according to the shekel of the sanctuary, and of olive oil a hin. You shall make of these a holy anointing oil, a perfume mixture, the work of a perfumer; it shall be a holy anointing oil. With it you shall anoint the tent of meeting and the ark of the testimony, and the table and all its utensils, and the lampstand and its utensils, and the altar of incense, and the altar of burnt offering and all its utensils, and the laver and its stand. You shall also consecrate them, that they may be most holy; whatever touches them shall be holy. You shall anoint Aaron and his sons, and consecrate them, that they may minister as priests to Me. You shall speak to the sons of Israel, saying, "This shall be a holy anointing oil to Me throughout your generations. It shall not be poured on anyone's body, nor shall you make any like it in the same proportions; it is holy, and it shall be holy to you. Whoever shall mix any like it or whoever puts any of it on a layman shall be cut off from his people"'" (Ex. 30:22-33, NASB).

Special oil for special moments! God required that Israel's perfumers create a unique fragrance for the sanctuary and its services, and in doing so, He coupled the aroma of this special substance with the powerful spiritual experience His people would have there in the sanctuary. Whenever you smelled that distinctive fragrance, you were to think of God. You were to sense the presence of the holy and be reminded of the tent of meeting where God would graciously receive His people. The Apocalypse retains this imagery of aroma even for the heavenly sanctuary (Rev. 5:8; 8:3, 4).

Scripture tells us that coupled with the anointing "the Spirit of the Lord came mightily upon David from that day forward" (1 Sam. 16:13, NASB). Simultaneous with the ceremony the Spirit arrived like a rushing wind. The Hebrew text reads that "the Spirit (wind) of the Lord rushed upon David from that day forward." The fragrant oil Samuel poured out served as the visible sign of the Spirit of God who, from that day forward, was to be upon David in mighty power. It pointed to an empowering for leadership and faithful service. Being anointed meant that God had given the person a job.[5] But more than that, it indicated that God had empowered the individual to do that very work. Anointing connects us with the work of God. The mission has a spiritual dimension to it, something that we cannot do unless filled with the Holy Spirit.

So this "shapeless, invasive fluid" of ceremonial oil represents God as actually being there. "As the oil worked its way in to the individual's hair and pores, it symbolized the divine presence entering into the one being anointed."[6] The alluring fragrance was part of the imagery. The Spirit would permeate the inner life—the heart. He would diffuse Himself through the person, bringing divine energy to everything that flowed from the heart. Thus the Spirit's sweet and gracious presence would affect every area of David's life and being. As one can smell Dolce Vita several rooms away, so the coming of the Spirit into his life was to be like a fragrance that invades one's inner space and haunts the imagination, leaving a telltale aroma that people notice and find themselves attracted to. Such is the work of the Holy Spirit upon the heart. God has a Dolce Vita—a beautiful life that diffuses and invades, creating a subtle passion hard to miss or ignore.

Unforgettable Contrasts

Thierry Wasser, a perfumer at Firmenich, tells how Cuir de Russie conjures memories of his late father. "My father always wore driving gloves," Wasser says, toying with a bottle of fragrance in front of him. "He would splash on his fragrance, pull on his gloves, and drive off. He left for good when I was 3. He died when I was 15. He pulled off the road in the south of France and slumped over the wheel. A heart attack. At 18 I learned to drive. I took out his gloves. When I put them on, the warmth of my hands released the scent of his cologne." Dipping a blotter into the bottle of Cuir de Russie he's been playing with, he waves it under his nose. "The ghost is in the bottle," he says.[7]

Memory—unleashed by a fragrance. Amazingly, a familiar perfume lingers in an old pair of gloves, conjuring up feelings and thoughts of a father. It is there to stay, just waiting for moist warm hands to release the scent.

"The Spirit of the Lord came mightily upon David from that day forward" (1 Sam. 16:13, NASB). I want you to catch the significance of the phrase *"from that day forward."* It speaks of power, purpose, and permanence. Then Scripture hits us with a shocking contrast that should jolt us every time we read it. Inconceivable back-to-back statements—"The Spirit of the Lord came mightily upon David from that day forward" and "Now the Spirit of the Lord departed from Saul, and an evil spirit from the Lord terrorized him" (verse 14, NASB). David's new status before the Lord stands in sharp contrast to Saul's. When the Lord rejected him as king (1 Sam. 15:23, 26; 16:1), "the Spirit of the Lord departed from Saul" (1 Sam. 16:14, NASB). Evidently he had "lost the empowering reality behind the anointing" that had marked his own selection for divine service years earlier (cf. 1 Sam. 10:1, 10).[8] Though God rejected Saul as king of Israel, He allowed him to rule for about four decades (1 Sam. 13:1). But Saul did so without God's presence or His power—surely without passion for God. It was many years of Spiritless leadership. Unfortunately, it's the tragic reality of so many. They spend years in God's work and church, living the Christian life, but devoid of the Spirit. It's a simple equation: no Holy Spirit, no passion.

In the course of time Saul became emotionally and spiritually burned out. Leadership-wise, he was in ruins. The same Spirit of the Lord that once motivated Saul now fills David. Scripture confronts us with the tension between the promise of the Spirit's enduring presence in our life and the reality that He can depart.

Even more troubling is the alarming comment telling how, when the Spirit of God departed from Saul, an evil spirit entered in its place. Here we encounter a puzzling question: How do we explain the evil spirit as coming from the Lord? Simply put, it means that when God withdrew His own Spirit, Satan was free to have his way. Old Testament Scripture usually portrays God as ultimately in charge. Satan works within the sphere of divine permission. The Lord simply allowed the exchange—evil spirit for Holy Spirit.

Redpath tells us that "whenever God's presence is withdrawn from a soul, when His Holy Spirit is taken away in His convicting power, that man is left in hopeless revolt against everything around him."[9] But even more so, such people leave themselves open to the controlling influence of the powers of darkness. As Ellen White notes: "Every man, woman, and child that is not under the control of the Spirit of God is under the influence of Satan's sorcery."[10] There is no such thing as a static heart. "We must be daily controlled by the Spirit of God or we are controlled by Satan."[11] The choice is ours.

The Spirit's Points of Entry

Scripture thus sets David and Saul side by side for our careful, thoughtful meditation. God had chosen both men for leadership. The Spirit had anointed both. But that is where comparison ceases and contrast begins. In this opening episode we see the sun begin to gloriously rise upon one life and to tragically set on the other. David's life exhibits a steady growth in grace and in the knowledge of God—passion for God. Saul displays a spiritual decline and mounting disobedience to God. His life becomes only darkness, frustration, and sin—emptied of any real passion except to destroy David.[12]

What made the difference? Why would the Spirit come to David and depart from Saul? How could David experience passion for God and Saul lose it altogether?

After he became king of Israel, Saul's actions and decisions soon revealed that he was a selfish, rash, angry, hateful, and mean-spirited individual. Eventually something snapped within, and during the later years of his rule he lost touch with reality—thus proving himself unqualified for the job. Not long after Saul's reign began, Samuel caught him in a serious act of disobedience. First, Israel's king didn't wait for Samuel before offering sacrifices to the Lord (1 Sam. 13). Wanting to keep his frightened, unproven army together and ready for battle, he feared that they would disperse if too much time passed before they engaged in battle.

Later Saul openly disobeyed God by not completely destroying the Amalekites and all that they possessed (1 Sam. 15). He returned from battle not only with the best of the cattle and possessions as spoils, but he had captured Agag, the Amalekite king, and brought him back alive as his biggest trophy. "Neither act of disobedience appeared sinful. Neither involved immorality or injustice. Both of them made perfect sense in terms of military strategy; in fact, both acts were dictated by good military strategy."[13] Saul simply thought he was doing the right thing.

When Samuel questioned the king about these things, Saul at first maintained that he had obeyed the voice of the Lord (verse 20). Pressed further, though, he began to rationalize what he had done, and then finally grudgingly admitted his disobedience. In the end Saul simply didn't see what all the fuss was about. He exhibited no repentance, no transformation of heart, no change of direction. In both cases people loomed larger in Saul's considerations than God did (1 Sam. 13:11, 12; 15:21, 24). The king was more concerned about his image and keeping his nation's loyalty than doing God's will and honoring Him. In fact, when you get right down to it, Saul wasn't that interested in God at all.[14]

Despite a promising start, the tenor of his life and leadership revealed a distinct lack of spiritual interest and meaningful relationship with the Lord. When you are not all that interested in God, you are not all that motivated to obey Him. Such lack of interest in God and obeying Him depletes spiritual passion. That's the bottom line of this narrative—an obedient heart. For if you have an obedience problem, you have a heart problem. And if you have a heart problem, the Spirit of the Lord will eventually depart and another spirit (demonic) will take His place. The pendulum of passion will swing accordingly. That's sobering! Samuel puts it this way: "What is more pleasing to the Lord: your burnt offerings and sacrifices or your obedience to his voice? Obedience is far better than sacrifice. Listening to him is much better than offering the fat of rams. Rebellion is as bad as the sin of witchcraft, and stubbornness is as bad as worshiping idols. So because you have rejected the word of the Lord, he has rejected you from being king" (1 Sam. 15:22, 23, NLT). Thus Samuel characterizes the passion of Saul's heart as rebellious and stubborn. The same spirit that fuels witchcraft and idolatry energizes disobedience.

Saul was anointed of the Lord but disobedient to the word of the Lord. For years God waited patiently for Saul to repent. But he didn't. By acting presumptuously in his dealing with the Amalekites, the king sealed his doom (verses 20-23).

David, however, was both interested in God and in obeying God. He had an *obedient heart*. Samuel alludes to this fact when he criticized Saul for his impatience: "You have acted foolishly; you have not kept the commandment of the Lord your God, which He commanded you, for now the Lord would have established your kingdom over Israel forever. But now your kingdom shall not endure. The Lord has sought out for Himself a man after His own heart, and the Lord has appointed him as ruler over His people, because you have not kept what the Lord commanded you" (1 Sam. 13:13, 14, NASB). Paul's commentary in Antioch on the Saul/David story states it point-blank: "After He had removed him [Saul], He raised up David to be their king, concerning whom He also testified and said, 'I have found David the son of Jesse, a man after My heart, *who will do all My will*'" (Acts 13:22, NASB).

Reading David's heart through his psalms reveals just how passionate he was about obeying God: "I delight to do thy will, O my God: yea, thy law is within my heart" (Ps. 40:8); "Teach me thy way, O Lord; I will walk in thy truth: unite my heart to fear thy name" (Ps. 86:11). The 176 verses of Psalm 119[15]—meditations and prayers relating to the word and will of God[16]—further amplify David's heart attitude about obedience. Listen to these explosive heart meditations about doing the will of God:

"With all my heart I have sought You; do not let me wander from Your commandments" (verse 10, NASB).

"Your word I have treasured in my heart, that I may not sin against You. Blessed are You, O Lord; teach me Your statutes" (verses 11, 12, NASB).

"I have rejoiced in the way of Your testimonies, as much as in all riches" (verse 14, NASB).

"I shall delight in Your statutes; I shall not forget Your word" (verse 16, NASB).

"Teach me, O Lord, the way of Your statutes, and I shall observe it to the end. Give me understanding, that I may observe Your law and keep it with all my heart. Make me walk in the path of Your commandments, for I delight in it. Incline my heart to Your testimonies and not to dishonest gain" (verses 33-36, NASB).

"O how I love Your law! It is my meditation all the day" (verse 97, NASB).

"I have inherited Your testimonies forever, for they are the joy of my heart. I have inclined my heart to perform Your statutes forever, even to the end" (verses 111, 112, NASB).

"My soul keeps Your testimonies, and I love them exceedingly" (verse 167, NASB).

In verse 32 David vows, "I shall run the way of Your commandments, for You will enlarge my heart" (NASB). David spent a lifetime living out Psalm 119—running in the ways of God so that he had an "enlarged heart" toward both life and God. Living large for God for a lifetime, he willingly yielded his heart in obedience to his God. Unlike many whose souls shrivel because of life's hardships, the lure of the world, or jading experiences with sin, David developed a fundamental attitude that literally expanded his soul—yielding himself in willful obedience to God. It reminds me of something Ellen White wrote: "All true obedience comes from the heart. It was heart work with Christ. And if we consent, He will so identify Himself with our thoughts and aims, so blend our hearts and minds into conformity to His will, that when obeying Him we shall be but carrying out our own impulses. The will, refined and sanctified, will find its highest delight in doing His service. When we know God as it is our privilege to know Him, our life will be a life of continual obedience."[17]

You cannot have passion if you are not willing to give yourself to wherever or whatever that passion has been awakened toward. And there can be no passion for God without yielding to His will. Passion not only claims it all—all the heart and soul and strength and mind—it presses the heart to yield it all as well. While (as with Saul) disobeying God depletes passion, the desire and choice to obey nurtures it. As David's experience and testimony suggest, passion for God engenders obedience. The opposite is true also—obeying God leads to passion for Him. Obedience is both the root and the fruit of passion for the Lord. Passion yielding to obedience enlarges the heart toward Him.

The gist of being a man or woman with a heart like His, then, comes down to passionate obedience (1 Sam. 13:14), of doing all of God's will (Acts 13:22). Obedience stems from the spiritual quality of our heart. We obey because we are interested in God, because He is important to us. And what we believe about Him further shapes our passion for Him. When you are not all that interested in God you have little desire to obey Him, and if you have an obedience problem, you have a heart problem. David loved God with all his heart, and because he loved Him with all his heart, he wanted to obey God from his heart as well. That's passion!

You Anoint My Head With Oil

"From that day on the Spirit of the Lord came upon David in power" (1 Sam. 16:13, NIV). "The Spirit of the Lord had left Saul, and the Lord sent a tormenting spirit that filled him with depression and fear" (verse 14, NLT). The back-to-back statements provide a shocking contrast that should startle us every time we read them. Scripture sets David's Spirit-empowered life in sharp contrast to Saul's utter emptiness of both Spirit and passion for God—and the astonishing consequences of depression, fear, and unceasing restlessness.

When I read sobering words like these, I cannot help wondering how many professing Christian people have no power in their witness, no radiance in their faces, no sweetness in their personalities, no reality in their spiritual lives—and no passion for God.[18] As Jesus said to the church at Sardis, "I know all the things you do, and that you have a reputation for being alive—but you are dead" (Rev. 3:1, NLT). And similarly to the Laodiceans: "I know all the things you do, that you are neither hot nor cold. I wish you were one or the other!" (verse 15, NLT). I both shudder at the possibility that Saul's experience might ever happen to me and find myself strangely drawn by the hope that I could have David's.

A few summers ago a raging windstorm ripped off the top third of a giant oak tree in our backyard. It was an outstretched tree reaching more than 80 feet toward the Michigan sky, full of large foliage-covered branches that spread in every direction. For the most part it was vertical, but eight or so feet from the ground a fork veered off the trunk, forming a lopsided V as it leaned well out over our house like a drooping flower. The listing offshoot was every bit as tall as the rest of the tree and exceeded two feet in diameter at its base.

The storm came with a cataract of rain so thick you couldn't see beyond the windows. Every tree around our wooded lot was in commotion. Astonishingly, the violent wind of the storm ripped off only the top 30 or so feet of the vertical section of this giant tree without so much as touching a tiny branch or single leaf of the portion that leaned out over our house. As I inspected the scene afterward, I couldn't figure it out. How could that mighty wind have ripped off just the top of the vertical section—as if it were just made of toothpicks—and then nicely dump all the debris on the back lawn without any damage to our home without so much as touching the equally as high section that leaned out over our house? Surely God's hedge of protection had surrounded my family that day.

Have you ever watched wind in the trees? How a single tree or a group of them will begin swaying with the wind while other trees right beside them remain untouched? Then suddenly the trees that are swaying with the wind still, and some of those previously motionless ones begin to stir? I've seen the wind dance all around one tree, yet whip in a frenzy every other tree around it. And I've seen just one tree swaying in the breeze while all those around it appeared perfectly still.

Wind is an exciting phenomenon and filled with mystery. Whenever I watch or feel wind blowing, I think of the Holy Spirit. Jesus Himself made the connection: "The wind blows wherever it pleases. You hear its sound, but you cannot tell where it comes from or where it is going. So it is with everyone born of the Spirit" (John 3:8, NIV). As the grass bends in the wind, water churns on a lake, clouds hurtle across the sky, or the breeze ruffles my hair, I consciously invite God's Spirit to blow through me. I've done it so many times now that it's almost automatic. The stronger the breeze, the more I find myself yearning for this mighty power of God (like a mighty rushing wind) to work in my life. It's an existential moment in which my heart and mind reach once again for the invisible God as the blowing wind stirs spiritual passion within me.

Just as the wind can dance around a given tree without touching it at all, yet shake every tree around it, so the Holy Spirit can work powerfully in a family or a church community's life while individuals in their midst remain untouched with the divine power or promptings. And just as a solitary tree can stir with the breeze while every other tree around it remains perfectly still, so the Holy Spirit can act on one person's heart and imagination while everyone else is oblivious to what God is doing. Why is it that a congregation can gather for worship and some within that fellowship feel the powerful awakening work of God's Spirit in their life while others sit there bored to death? Some experience the Spirit's presence and power while others know nothing of His work in their lives? How can it be?

Rick was part of a home Bible fellowship. The dozen or so who gathered each week to explore Scripture and pray together decided one night to begin studying the Holy Spirit. They had come to the end of a study series and were considering various topics for their next round. For some reason, they kept gravitating toward the theme of the Holy Spirit. Rick tells how at first no one really wanted to spend so much time on the subject. It seemed too mystical and not particularly relevant. He especially wasn't interested. But somehow the group felt led to the topic and began their nearly three-month journey learning all they could about the Holy Spirit.

Somewhere along the way Rick realized something was happening deep within himself. He had always thought of the Holy Spirit as the "Comforter" or "Helper." Someone there to help and strengthen and to reveal the meaning of Scripture. But now he was experiencing the Holy Spirit as the "Spirit of Truth." The third member of the Godhead was shining a pretty bright spotlight into some buried corners of his heart, pointing out things he hadn't given too much thought about. One day Rick faced the startling reality that he had really yielded only 90 percent of his heart to God. That other 10 percent now began to awaken as the Spirit plowed through his heart. And he struggled with a tortured dilemma—letting go of that remaining 10 percent meant surrendering some attitudes and feelings and behaviors that had either been off limits to God or not all that unimportant in his scheme of things. Only by yielding could he experience the promised fullness of the Spirit. A battle raged within him as pride and self-control fought to maintain their mastery. But the desire for the fullness of the Spirit continued to grow. Rick tells of that day of decision when he gave himself completely to God, confessing his sins and asking God to remove certain things from his heart and life. "When I asked God to take those things out of my life, He did. And then He filled the vacuum with the Holy Spirit." From that moment Rick's passion for God became undeniable to those who know him.

Although the Holy Spirit had departed from Saul, years later God gave him an incredible opportunity to regain the Spirit. It happened when David ran for protection from the king to the prophet Samuel at Ramah. At Ramah Samuel presided over a school of prophets—something on the order of a monastery of prophets living in a cluster of dwellings. There the prophets immersed themselves in a daily round of praying, studying God's

Word, and prophesying (1 Sam. 19:18-20).[19] Believing that Saul would not order his troops to invade the sacred place, David thus claimed sanctuary.[20]

Sanctuary or not, Saul immediately sent a posse to capture David and bring him back to the palace. When the king's officers arrived, they found themselves caught up in prophetic ecstasies and overwhelmed by God's Spirit. In the process they forgot their order to arrest David (verse 20). They spent the day singing and praying instead. When Saul heard what happened, instead of feeling God's rebuke he dispatched more men to capture David. The same thing happened to the second squad (verse 21). In his unabated hostility and determination, Saul ordered a third company of men after the fugitive—only to have the Spirit of God fill them as well and stop them from capturing David (verse 21). The story builds in dramatic power by the thrice-repeated statement about messengers arriving who find themselves grasped by the Spirit and as a result begin prophesying.[21]

By now Saul, thoroughly disgusted, decides to take matters into his own hands. Murder on his mind, he too goes to Ramah. But his evil intent is no better able to withstand God's Spirit than his soldiers had been. He soon falls completely under the influence of God's Spirit and gives witness to God's presence by praying, singing, and prophesying (verses 22, 23). The Spirit has seized the king so powerfully that he strips off his clothes and lies naked before Samuel all that day and through the night (verse 24). The compelling, inscrutable, inexplicable power of the Holy Spirit renders the king helpless.[22] This spell of goodness makes him temporarily incapable of evil.[23] Bowing in submission, he prays, sings, prophesys, and talks of God.

While some details in the incident elude our understanding, the thrust of the story is clear enough. God was demonstrating His "power to make even a demon-dominated man act like a righteous person."[24] In the process, the Lord communicated a vital message to Saul. He was reminding him of a very special event earlier in his life when Samuel had anointed him king and the Spirit came upon him so mightily that he prophesied among the prophets (1 Sam. 10:10). Now it happens again. "God was saying, loud and clear, that he was still able to change Saul's heart and life permanently—if only Saul would let Him."[25]

"Look what I can do, Saul," God tells him. "I can make you bow down in submission to Me. I can make songs of praise flow from your lips. And

I can compel you to pray and prophesy. All with fervency, zeal—passion. Now I'm doing it again to show you that I am still able. But this Spirit-empowered experience will last only these 24 hours—unless you choose Me again, wholeheartedly, by yielding your all to Me once and for all. For while I can make you act like a righteous person now (and forever, for that matter), I will neither force your will nor take away your freedom to choose. It's up to you, Saul. I'm here. My Spirit waits for you to yield it all."

The Lord was reaching out to the king, giving him an incredible opportunity to restore his spiritual passion. But when God withdrew His Spirit after that 24-hour phenomenon, Saul was just as passionless for Him as before. He refused to yield, spurning the moment of divine demonstration and invitation.

The Spirit's entry inevitably comes with a price—an obedient heart. Spirit-anointed passion for God yields it all! There must be radical self-emptying,[26] full surrender to the Word and will and claims of God on one's life. It's a biblical principle—God gives the Holy Spirit only to those who obey (or are willing to obey) Him (Acts 5:32; see 1 Peter 1:2). That's how David came to both experience and understand it. His psalms speak so eloquently and frequently about obedience because he had personally learned how it both sustains and nurtures passion. And Saul's experience so indelibly impressed itself on David's young mind that years later, when he sinned with Bathsheba, he was terribly afraid that he might lose God's Spirit because of his sins. Consequently, when he failed God, David prayed that the Lord would not take His Holy Spirit from him (Ps. 51:11).

God gives the Holy Spirit only to those who obey. It's a simple link that we can view from differing perspectives: no obedience, no Holy Spirit, no passion. No Holy Spirit, no obedience, no passion. No Holy Spirit, no passion, no obedience. Or no passion, no obedience, no Holy Spirit. As Meyer writes: "The blessed anointing for service cannot be ours unless there has been a previous gracious work on the heart. There must be the new life—the life of God. There must be submission of heart, humility, faithfulness to duty, cleansing from known sin, and a close walk with God. The descending flame must fall on the whole burnt offering of a consecrated life."[27]

Asked whether he was filled with the Spirit, Dwight L. Moody replied, "Yes. But I leak." Every one of us can identify with that reality. We too leak. The Spirit is either grieved, quiet, distant, absent, or departing. And it happens too often. Disobedience, refusing to yield it all, and being content with halfhearted, lukewarm, passionless spiritual existence all cause our passion to drain out of our lives. As Ellen White asserts: "When one is fully emptied of self, when every false god is cast out of the soul, the vacuum is filled by the inflowing of the Spirit of Christ."[28] There is either inflowing or outgoing, passion or lukewarmness. And self-emptying is the key. An obedient heart that yields it all is what passion for God is really all about. But we cannot do this work of self-emptying on our own. We do not have the power—only desire and choice. "No outward observances can take the place of simple faith and entire renunciation of self. But no man can empty himself of self. We can only consent for Christ to accomplish the work. Then the language of the soul will be, Lord, take my heart; for I cannot give it. It is Thy property. Keep it pure, for I cannot keep it for Thee. Save me in spite of myself, my weak, unchristlike self. Mold me, fashion me, raise me into a pure and holy atmosphere, where the rich current of Thy love can flow through my soul."[29] Only then can there be Dolce Vita—a beautiful Spirit-filled life that diffuses and invades every part of us. It alone will give us a subtle passion for God that's hard to miss or ignore.

Passion yields it all! Are you willing to pay that kind of price for passion? Are you willing to ask God right now to take your heart and fill you with His Spirit?

---

[1] Cathy Newman, "Perfume, the Essence of Illusion," *National Geographic* (October 1998), pp. 94-119.

[2] Although some posit that David's conspicuous absence supports the theory that Jesse knew why Samuel had come. Would not God choose the son with the greatest physical stature and chronological maturity? After all, Saul was the tallest man in Israel and his replacement would surely need to be someone like him.

[3] Ellen G. White, *Patriarchs and Prophets*, p. 641. The Hebrew word קֶרֶב (*qereb*), translated "midst," denotes the internal. It can represent the inward part(s) of human or animal bodies, or of groups of people, or of social structures. It frequently functions as a preposition "in the midst, among" (Hab. 3:2; Num. 14:13). David was anointed "from among" his brothers. "The rite took place in the presence of his brothers, that is, privately, or even secretly. Presumably this would help explain why other people . . . were unaware of it. Even Eliab, his brother, seemed to be ignorant of David's anointing in 17:28" (Ralph W. Klein, *1 Samuel*, p. 162).

[4] The Hebrew word for anoint מָשַׁח (*māshah*) has a fourfold theological significance. First, to anoint an individual or an object indicated an authorized separation or setting apart for God's service (Lev. 8:12; cf. Ex. 29:36 for the altar). The expression "anointed to the

Lord" (1 Chron. 29:22), while representing a position of honor, also represents increased responsibility. Second, though the agent doing the anointing might be the priest or prophet, writers speak of anointed ones as those whom the Lord anointed (e.g., 1 Sam. 10:1; 2 Sam. 12:7). Such language underscores that it is God who is the authorizing agent; that the anointed is inviolable (1 Sam. 24:8ff.); and that the anointed one is to be held in special regard (cf. 1 Sam. 26:9ff.). Third, one may infer that people understood divine enablement as accompanying an anointing. Scripture says of both Saul and David in connection with their anointing that "the Spirit of God came mightily upon him" (1 Sam. 10:6ff.; 1 Sam. 16:13ff.). Finally, Scripture associated the notion of the "anointed one" מָשִׁיחַ (māshîah) with the coming promised deliverer, i.e., the Messiah. The prospect of a righteous, Spirit-filled ruler increasingly appears in the Old Testament (cf. Isa. 9:1-7; 11:1-5; 61:1).

[5] Eugene Peterson, *Leap Over a Wall: Earthly Spirituality for Everyday Christians* (New York: HarperSanFrancisco, 1998), p. 28.

[6] Robert D. Bergen, *1, 2 Samuel,* p. 180.

[7] Newman, p. 102.

[8] Bergen, p. 182.

[9] Alan Redpath, *The Making of a Man of God: Studies in the Life of David* (Grand Rapids: Fleming H. Revell, 1994), p. 34.

[10] Ellen G. White, *Messages to Young People* (Nashville: Southern Pub. Assn., 1930), p. 278.

[11] _____, *Testimonies for the Church* (Mountain View, Calif.: Pacific Press Pub. Assn., 1948), vol. 5, p. 102.

[12] Redpath, p. 31.

[13] Peterson, p. 26.

[14] *Ibid.*

[15] Psalm 119 is unique in Scripture. The longest psalm, it alludes to many other scriptures in its 176 verses. The 22 stanzas each consist of eight verses, and each commences with a letter of the Hebrew alphabet.

[16] The prominent designation for Scripture in Psalm 119 is "word," which in turn has seven designations—way, law, testimonies, precepts, statutes, judgments, and commandments.

[17] Ellen G. White, *The Desire of Ages* (Mountain View, Calif.: Pacific Press Pub. Assn., 1898), p. 668.

[18] Redpath, p. 17.

[19] Peterson, p. 56. The word *Naioth* (1 Sam. 19:18) literally means "dwellings/habitations" and may refer to a religious compound within Ramah (Bergen, pp. 209, 210).

[20] White, *Patriarchs and Prophets,* p. 653.

[21] Walter Brueggemann, *First and Second Samuel, Interpretation, A Bible Commentary for Teaching and Preaching* (Louisville, Ky.: John Knox Press, 1990), p. 144.

[22] Brueggemann, p. 145.

[23] Peterson, p. 56.

[24] Keith Kaynor, *When God Chooses: The Life of David,* p. 70.

[25] Eugene A. Getz, *David: Seeking God Faithfully,* p. 90. See White, *Patriarchs and Prophets,* pp. 653, 654.

[26] Ellen G. White, *Gospel Workers* (Washington, D.C.: Review and Herald Pub. Assn., 1948), p. 287.

[27] F. B. Meyer, *The Life of David,* pp. 17, 18.

[28] White, *Gospel Workers,* p. 287.

[29] _____, *Christ's Object Lessons* (Washington, D.C.: Review and Herald Pub. Assn., 1900), p. 159.

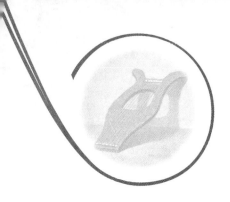

3

SOFT MUSIC FOR A HARD HEART

I Samuel 16:14-23

It was the beginning of Act I of a live broadcast of Rossini's *Barber of Seville* from the Metropolitan Opera House in New York. Lorna was driving home on a rainy afternoon when a truck rear-ended her just before the woman playing Rosina was to sing.

"The impact was sudden and stunning," recalled the self-possessed New Jersey professional. "But even as I entered a world of shock and pain, I found a world of bliss and order. I listened to the whole aria and the next 15 minutes of the opera as ambulance people and firemen tried to free me from the wreckage of my car." State emergency crews later told her that she had been unconscious until they strapped her into a cot in the ambulance, but she remembered listening to Rosina's voice throughout the ordeal. "The music kept me alive," she says. "I was able to listen and stay conscious, alert, and at peace with the music. I never thought I was injured, because the music was so alive. I just kept listening, listening. From the beginning of the aria, I knew I had to finish the opera of my life."[1]

Can music really pull us through crises? Can it actually reorder our inner world, bringing us peace, hope, and healing? The servants of Saul seemed to think so. "Now the Spirit of the Lord departed from Saul, and an evil spirit from the Lord terrorized him. Saul's servants then said to him, 'Behold now, an evil spirit from God is terrorizing you. Let our lord now command your servants who are before you. Let them seek a man who is a skillful player on the harp; and it shall come about when the evil spirit from God is on you, that he shall play the harp with his hand, and you will be well'" (1 Sam. 16:14-16, NASB).

Such passages provide insight into how the ancients understood the power and value of music. They knew how to use it to promote harmony and well-being in their lives. For them music was not just a form of entertainment—it was also a source of health, containing chords of rhythm and melody that harmonized and rebalanced the human organism, draining away its impurities.[2] They believed that "music soothed passions, healed mental diseases, and even held in check riots and tumults."[3]

Here we encounter King Saul with his strange malady—a terrorizing evil spirit from the Lord. The Hebrew word for terrorizing is bā'at, which means "to fall upon, to startle, to overwhelm." I imagine people spooked by a sudden hair-raising encounter, such as a fiend hiding silently in the shadows and suddenly lunging out of nowhere, scaring the life out of them. Perhaps they are in a haunted house and every creak and shadow or movement holds unknown terrors. Saul imagines something dark and evil lurking behind the seen—everywhere, incessantly—until he's paranoid. Old Testament scholars C. F. Keil and F. Delitzsch suggest that his experience "was not merely an inward feeling of depression at the rejection announced to him, which grew into melancholy, and occasionally broke out in passing fits of insanity, but a higher evil power, which took possession of him, and not only deprived him of his peace of mind, but stirred up the feelings, ideas, imagination, and thoughts of his soul to such an extent that at times it drove him even into madness."[4] Feelings of guilt and separation from God no doubt aggravated Saul's torments. The soul bereft of the Spirit of God has no peace. He was constantly occupied, too, with anticipating the ruin that Samuel promised would come to his leadership and family. When and how would it happen? In that era leadership transition was often brutal and bloody. Saul sensed it meant doom for his family.

Whatever caused it, Saul's affliction would come and go (1 Sam. 16:16, 23) and was so obvious to those around him that even his servants realized he needed help. So they boldly suggested their treatment—music therapy. Three important criteria guided their thinking. First, it needed to be a certain kind of music. As a general rule, different instruments affect particular parts of our makeup—physical body, emotions, soul, mind. This was no time for percussion, brass, or the heavy sound of bass notes. Saul was already being harshly jerked around and pounded from within. The servants imagine, rather, the gentle haunting rhythms of a hand-stroked string instrument—the *kinnôr,* a musical instrument having strings and a wooden frame. We'd call it a harp. Harp music has long been known for its haunting, soul-touching gentleness and rhythms.[5]

Second, the musician needed to be highly skilled—someone who, when they played, would immediately capture the king's attention and touch him deep down within. Saul's servants were concerned with the artistry of rhythm and interpretation that elicits a spontaneous response from the hearer. It was something that only an accomplished musician could bring off. Finally, this maestro needed to be someone whose personal life and ethic conveyed the influence and presence of God. They didn't exactly spell that out at first, but it was on their mind. When Saul said "Provide for me now a man who can play well and bring him to me" (1 Sam. 16:17, NASB), one of his servants immediately had a suggestion. "I have seen," he says, "a son of Jesse the Bethlehemite who is a skillful musician, a mighty man of valor, a warrior, one prudent in speech, and a handsome man; and the Lord is with him" (verse 18, NASB). Now that's not a bad résumé, is it?

David was a skilled musician, a man of valor, a warrior, someone who had control of his tongue, was handsome, and the Lord was with him. What we need to see here is the conscious blend of art and heart, character and musicianship, and music and the music maker. Evidently the servant had heard him play and had felt the spiritual power of his music. He knew David had the tenderness and the sensitivity of an artist as well as the character and spiritual depth needed to lift Saul out of his melancholy moods. His servants evidently understood the spiritual nature of the king's malady and knew the kind of music that would make a difference.

The music that Saul's servants had in mind was not just any kind played by anybody on just any type of instrument. Well aware of music that could open the door to unclean spirits, they wanted music animated by nobler inspiration and that would elevate the soul by its harmonious melody. As Krummacher notes: "They recommended to him the power of music as a means of relieving his mind, but with a wise discriminating judgment regarding its character. There was, indeed, no lack of musicians at the court at Gibeah; but they appear to have been devoid of the qualifications which were at this time needed. The servants knew well the power of music to produce, according to its kind and quality, not less than the most destructive passions; but it can also, at least momentarily, tame and mitigate the wildest storms of the human heart."[6]

As it turned out, David's music was effective. "Whenever the spirit from God was upon Saul, . . . David would take a harp and play it with his hand. Then Saul would become refreshed and well, and the distressing spirit would depart from him" (verse 23, NKJV). Moffatt puts it this way: He played for Saul "till Saul breathed freely." Can you imagine someone so terrified that his adrenaline has peaked, his heart rate is running wild, and his breathing is rapid and heavy? Now with the gentle rhythms of soft music, he relaxes and breathes freely. Somehow David's music made an unmistakable difference. It brought relief. By the time he left him, Saul was unburdened, and the evil presence had departed.[7]

The shepherd-musician provided soft music for a hard heart, chords of comfort. Ellen White tells us that "his lofty and heaven-inspired strains had the desired effect. The brooding melancholy that had settled like a dark cloud over the mind of Saul was charmed away."[8] While David was obviously a skilled musician, his success in bringing relief for Saul resulted from the fact that the Spirit of the Lord was with him in power (verses 13, 18).[9] More was at work here than art. Talent alone could not have soothed Saul's torment. Nor mere music. David chose melodies that ministered to the aching soul. But more important, his music was heaven-inspired, because as a music maker his heart was filled with the Holy Spirit. When the music maker is in touch with the creator of music, there will be unmistakable spiritual/moral power and artistry in their creation or performance.

The Mozart Effect

So we're confronted with the incredible healing power of music. It is more than just an ancient belief. The healing transforming power of music is a fact! Here we must deal with the ethics of music as well—the link between art and heart. We quickly learn that music is not neutral.[10] Likewise, instrumentation is an important consideration in terms of context and purpose. Excellence in musicianship is also essential. And the personal moral and spiritual experience of the music maker is indispensable.

Whatever our individual tastes might be, something about music powerfully touches our lives. It's a medium that moves, enchants, energizes, and heals us. But it can also jar and twist, filling us with gloomy thoughts, distract us, and saturate our mind with undesirable propaganda. (I think of all the unforgettable trash music ditties that rivet themselves in our minds and the banal and often downright immoral associations certain lyrics and tunes incessantly press upon our consciousness—and which we can never seem to erase from our minds. Sometimes I wish I had never heard certain things or connected with the real meaning of a piece of music.) In an instant, music can uplift our soul, awakening in us the spirit of prayer, compassion, and love. Or it can create a spirit of independence, rebellion, and anger. Music vanishes our blues or conjures up memories of lost lovers and deceased friends. It lets the child in us play, the monk in us pray, and the hero in us surmount all obstacles. Not only can it march us off to war; it helps the stroke patient find language and expression.

How does music affect us? It can mask unpleasant sounds and feelings and slow down and equalize brain waves. Besides affecting the heartbeat, pulse rate, and blood pressure, it can reduce muscle tension and improve body movement and coordination. Music can alter body temperature, increase endorphin levels (the brain's own "opiates") in the brain, regulate stress-related hormones, and boost the immune function. In addition, music can change our perceptions of space and time, strengthen memory and learning, boost productivity, and enhance romance and sexuality. Fostering endurance, it can generate a sense of safety and well-being. In the religious realm, music can build faith or tear it down, drawing us closer to God or pushing us headlong into evil.[11]

After reviewing hundreds of empirically based studies between 1972 and 1992, three educators associated with the Future of Music Project found that music instruction aided reading, language (including foreign language) skills, and mathematics skills as well as improving overall academic achievement. The research also found that music increased student creativity, self-esteem, and social skills, and increased perceptual motor skill development and psychomotor development.[12] The authors call music's impact "The Mozart Effect."

The pulse, pace, and pattern of music can either heal or distort. How we use music, the way we come to it, and the orientation of our heart when we create, use, or hear it are all important.

The inarguable power of music has demonstrated itself since before the foundation of our earth (Job 38:4-7). When God responded to Lucifer's questions regarding Christ's status among the heavenly host (before war literally broke out in heaven, Rev. 12:7-9), He summoned the heavenly host before Him to explain the true nature and position of His Son. Afterward "the angels joyfully acknowledged the supremacy of Christ, and prostrating themselves before Him, poured out their love and adoration. Lucifer bowed with them, but in his heart there was a strange, fierce conflict. Truth, justice, and loyalty were struggling against envy and jealousy. The influence of the holy angels seemed for a time to carry him with them. As songs of praise ascended in melodious strains, swelled by thousands of glad voices, the spirit of evil seemed vanquished; unutterable love thrilled his entire being; his soul went out, in harmony with the sinless worshipers, in love to the Father and the Son."[13]

Unfortunately, though, pride in his own glory again filled Lucifer's heart. His desire for supremacy returned, and he once more indulged envy of Christ. Ellen White tells us that "Satan had led the heavenly choir. He had raised the first note; then all the angelic host had united with him, and glorious strains of music had resounded through heaven in honor of God and His dear Son."[14] Satan well understands the power of music and uses it effectively for his purposes. Through it he can elicit mystical experiences, produce the illusion of religious sentiment, lure people to participate in false worship, and tear down faith and push one headlong into evil (Dan. 3:4-7, 10, 15; Ex. 32:6, 18; Num. 25:1, 2).

David's experience, however, suggests that music can also facilitate the rhythms of faith and healing. *The Desire of Ages* has a fascinating chapter on the early years of Jesus. There we read that Jesus—the "Son of David"—"often . . . expressed the gladness of His heart by singing psalms and heavenly songs. Often the dwellers in Nazareth heard His voice raised in praise and thanksgiving to God. He held communion with heaven in song; and as His companions complained of weariness from labor, they were cheered by the sweet melody from His lips. His praise seemed to banish the evil angels, and, like incense, fill the place with fragrance. The minds of His hearers were carried away from their earthly exile, to the heavenly home."[15]

Author Anne Lamott tells how, against all odds, she finally came to believe in God. Part of her troubled journey from damaged emotions and alcoholism to sobriety, emotional equilibrium, and God involved the gospel music emanating from an impoverished, ramshackle church right across the street from a Sunday flea market she frequented. The music wafting out so entranced her that she'd stop and listen even from across the street. After a while Anne found herself standing in the doorway to listen to the songs. It was a rundown place, with terrible brown and overshined linoleum and plastic "stained-glass" windows. But the people sang. Scared stiff that anyone would try to con her into coming in and sitting down, Anne kept her distance. But the singing nevertheless pulled her in and split her spiritually wide open. Soon she was singing too—from the doorway.

After a few months Anne took a seat in one of the folding chairs, off by herself. And, as she writes, "Then the singing enveloped me. It was furry and resonant, coming from everyone's very heart. There was no sense of performance or judgment, only that the music was breath and food. Something inside me that was stiff and rotting would feel soft and tender. Somehow the singing wore down all the boundaries and distinctions that kept me so isolated. Sitting there, standing with them to sing, sometimes so shaky and sick that I felt like I might tip over, I felt bigger than myself, like I was being taken care of, tricked into coming back to life. But I had to leave before the sermon."

One Sunday, Anne came to church so hung over that she couldn't stand up for the songs. This time she stayed for the sermon, which she thought was just utterly ridiculous—like someone trying to convince her that extraterrestrials really existed. But the last song was so deep and raw and pure that she could not escape. "It was as if the people were singing in between the notes," she recalls, "weeping and joyful at the same time, and I felt like their voices or *something* was rocking me in its bosom, holding me like a scared kid, and I opened up to that feeling—and it washed over me." Anne began to cry and left before the benediction. Racing home she felt as if a little cat were running along at her heels, wanting her to reach down and pick it up, wanting her to open the door to her house and let it in. She knew what would happen: you let a cat in one time, give it a little milk, and then it stays forever. Instinctively she knew that metaphorical cat was Jesus. When she arrived home she stood at the door and hung her head, thinking, *&#@~ * : I quit.* Then taking a long, deep breath, she said out loud, "All right. You can come in." It was her beautiful moment of conversion.[16]

Bill Moyer's documentary film on the hymn "Amazing Grace" includes a scene filmed in Wembley Stadium in London. Various musical groups, mostly rock bands, had gathered together in celebration of the incredible social changes that had just taken place in South Africa. For some reason the promoters scheduled an opera singer, Jessye Norman, for the closing act. For 12 hours groups such as Guns N' Roses blasted the unruly crowd through banks of speakers riling up fans already high on booze and dope. As the day progressed, the crowd yelled for more, and the rock groups obliged.

Finally the time came for Jessye to sing. As she strolled onstage, a single circle of light followed her. She had no backup band, no musical instruments, no flashing colored lights to dazzle imagination, just Jessye—a majestic African-American woman wearing a flowing African dashiki. Few recognized the opera star, and the crowd became restless. A voice yelled for more Guns N' Roses. Others took up the cry. Things were beginning to get ugly.

Then alone, and a cappella, Jessye Norman began singing, very slowly: "'Amazing grace! how sweet the sound, that saved a wretch like me! I once was lost, but now am found, was blind, but now I see.'"

As she sang, something remarkable began to happen—70,000 raucous fans fell silent before her aria of grace. By the time Norman reached the second verse, "''Twas grace that taught my heart to fear, and grace my fears relieved . . .'" the soprano held the crowd in her hands. And when she reached the final verse, "''Tis grace hath brought me safe thus far, and grace will lead me home,'" several thousand fans were singing along—digging far back in nearly lost memories for words they had heard long ago.

Jessye Norman later confessed she had no idea what power descended on Wembley Stadium that night. The answer, though, shouldn't be that hard to find. Our world thirsts for grace. When grace descends, the world falls silent before it, and when grace grips the heart, the people begin to sing![17] And when such amazing grace (or any truth of God, for that matter) is conveyed through awesomely beautiful music—performed even by an opera diva who may not be personally changed by such truth—it is powerful to transform lives and nurture faith.

Israel's Sweet Singer

You may not know him well, or not even have heard of him, for that matter, but Itzhak Perlman is an affable round-faced down-to-earth Jew with a ready smile who captures the heart of audiences worldwide with his music. Acclaimed as one of the twentieth century's greatest violin virtuosos, this gentle man has instant rapport with ordinary people. Perlman has a physical disability. He wobbles onstage while hanging on to special arm-support crutches. Then he kind of throws himself down on a chair (sometimes he plays from a wheelchair). Someone else carries his violin and waits until Perlman puts his crutches down and is ready to play. Perlman's so unassuming you begin to wonder if he's really a musician. Most of us would be embarrassed watching him. But when Perlman touches his bow to his violin you are lost in amazement at the enthusiasm and power and beauty of his music.

My wife had the opportunity to see Perlman at his best. Following a superb performance with the South Bend Symphony Orchestra, Perlman stood up on his crutches and wobbled away. As he exited, the audience stood for applause. When he reached the curtain on the side of the stage Perlman slipped and fell, crutches flying, legs collapsing, and arms flailing. For a moment he lay there scrambling to get up. The audience gasped, but kept applauding. Moments later his pianist returned, stating that Perlman was fine. Then, to everyone's surprise, Perlman once again wobbled onstage and played five captivating encores. Needless to say, he endeared himself even more deeply to that thunderously applauding crowd.

"What does all this have to do with David?" you ask. Scripture calls him "the sweet psalmist of Israel" (2 Sam. 23:1). Music was not just a passion in his life; it was an integral expression of his passion for God. He had a vision for its use in the worship of God and for expressing both personal and communal faith. David was so passionate and effective with music that he not only endeared himself to his people, but left a music legacy that would touch generations.

An illuminating detail about David's passion for music appears in the fact that he was a skilled musician tending sheep! "Send me your son David who is with the flock," Saul said to Jesse (1 Sam. 16:19, NASB). Don't miss those last five words—"who is with the flock." After being anointed king, David went right back to the sheep. Shepherding was rough, lonely work. It kept David out of the way, mostly ignored, with a lot of time on his hands. "The way he responded to the loneliness of a shepherd's life is a model for all who feel ignored and forgotten. Left alone, David used the time to full advantage. He developed his music ability. . . . This musical gift—this disciplined skill—would be God's vehicle for taking him into the highest circles of the land."[18] Ultimately his music would transform the worship experience of Israel and affect believers through the ages till Jesus comes. David was a young man with a passion for excellence in music. Here's a guy who knew the discipline of practice and the difference between mediocrity and precision. How else could he have been such a good shot with a sling? so skilled on the harp?

Keith Kaynor observes that besides his musical interests, "David had a sensitive and appreciative spirit. He had a thoughtful, contemplative heart. He was always thinking. It enabled him to capture in words his outlook on life. Writing as a third party and looking at his soul through a spiritual microscope, he had a unique ability to see life from God's perspective and to record God's viewpoint."[19] That's what we find in the poetry of his psalms. *Patriarchs and Prophets* tells us that he composed his own songs, which he sang to the accompaniment of his harp.[20] "The love that moved him, the sorrows that beset him, the triumphs that attended him, were all themes for his active thought; and as he beheld the love of God in all the providences of his life, his heart throbbed with more fervent adoration and gratitude, his voice rang out in a richer melody, his harp was swept with more exultant joy."[21]

Talk about passion! David was more than a technically skilled musician—his heart was caught up in the experience. Music became a form of both expressing his inner self and communicating his relationship with God. It served as a forum for riveting truths about God and life in his imagination. This passion with music extended throughout the entirety of his life.

While playing for Saul, David learned the effective power of music to both transform people's lives and awaken or nurture passion for God. Israel's future king realized that music had such powerful moral/spiritual force that when he became king, he elevated it to the highest level in the experience of his people. He appointed qualified people to prophesy or speak authoritatively for God accompanied by music (1 Chron. 25:1-3). Prophesying was explicitly connected with music and the use of musical instruments.[22] One gets the sense that the music both inspired the words spoken and served as a background to them. It certainly was a forum for expressing both the truth from or about God and of passion for God.

David also selected musicians to minister in the sanctuary and for the worship experience of the people. "Then David spoke to the chiefs of the Levites to appoint their relatives the singers, with instruments of music, harps, lyres, loud-sounding cymbals, to raise sounds of joy" (1 Chron. 15:16, NASB; see also 16:1-6, 42). He organized musicians and singers for the Temple that his son Solomon would eventually build. Altogether "the Levites were numbered from thirty years old and upward, and their number by census of men was 38,000. Of these, 24,000 were to oversee the work of the house of the Lord; and 6,000 were officers and judges, and 4,000 were gatekeepers, and 4,000 were praising the Lord with the instruments which David made for giving praise" (1 Chron. 23:3-5, NASB). David's vision for music included singers as well as instrumentalists. The musical instruments he used include the full repertoire of his day—percussion (castanet, tambourine, timbrel, and triangle); strings (harp, lute, lyre, and 10-stringed instruments); and winds (flute, horn, and trumpet).

Even more important is the fact that David chose leaders for the music (1 Chron. 25:1-7). "Chenaniah, chief of the Levites, was in charge of the singing; he gave instruction in singing because he was skillful" (1 Chron. 15:22, NASB). Such musicians were ministers of music supported by the people's tithe. Their task was to lead and train in worship. While they demanded excellence, they had more than performance in mind. The music was an act of worship, and the musicians were leading that worship.

Martin Luther wrote: "Next to the Word of God, music deserves the highest praise." He believed that the Reformation would not be complete until the saints of God had two things in their possession: a Bible in their own tongue, and a hymnal, which the Reformers called a Psalter. Taking a cue from David, Luther believed that they needed the Book that could lead them to a deeper understanding of their faith and a companion volume that would help them express with joy and pathos the depths of that faith.[23]

David thus was not only a skilled musician; he understood the power of music for worship—its ability to express the soul's personal journey and to articulate how wonderful and majestic and gracious the living God of heaven really is. Clearly he also understood, too, how music leadership was necessary for public worship. When I see how society spends literally billions of dollars each year on music for advertisements, or for creating atmosphere for social gatherings, entertainment, and movies, I can only ask, "Should not the church of Jesus Christ invest a similar energy and passion and dollars for music that will glorify the living God, build faith, heal hearts, and facilitate community in worship?"

No wonder Scripture calls David "Israel's sweet singer."

Art and Heart

One summer I sneaked out into the backyard to pitch a tent I had repeatedly promised to put up for my four sons. Although they had been wanting to sleep out in the backyard for some time, I kept procrastinating. But they kept insisting. Now the weather bureau had forecast a few really nice days, so I decided to surprise them while they were busy in their room playing with Matchbox cars and Legos. I figured I could set the tent up and then just casually ask, "What's that in the backyard?" Then I wanted to watch them run to the window and catch the expression on their faces when it all registered. It was one of those instant successes that make daddies wonder why they don't do things like that more often. Their excitement exhilarated me.

One response forever etched itself in my mind. It was the joyful abandon of our then 3-year-old Ethan. He wasted no time in getting his pajamas on. Soon he was racing in circles in the yard, leaping and running for all his worth, his thick locks of hair waving in the breeze. His eyes squinting with glee, he had a smile that wrapped itself to his ears. I stopped stuffing sleeping bags in the tent and stood to watch and listen. It was captivating. "I'm so happy! I'm so happy! I'm so happy!" he sang again and again as he raced round and round. It was a scene of sweet innocence and spontaneous celebration. Passion! Just because Daddy pitched a tent. As I said, it was the kind of experience that made me wonder why I get so busy with other things. That night as I lay in the darkness I thought about the carefree abandon of a heart bursting with joy and gladness. Filled with an experience that stirred his little heart, Ethan could not stop the passion that overflowed or the singing it induced.

David shared an experience with God that stirred his heart and also overflowed with passion. That passion for God elicited melodic creativity—singing and music-making. That's because passion by nature is imaginative. It fills the heart with art. Passion elicits creativity. When you have passion your imagination kicks in. Nothing is boring or colorless. Rather, there comes inspiration, vision, creativity, and freshness—the pursuit of excellence. You want to dance. Imagination has a way of making things different, better, fuller, richer, brand-new—all because one has both interest and enthusiasm about what one is either doing or experiencing. Passion connects directly with the right brain—both stimulating it and flowing from it—thus its imaginative power.

People with passion have a thousand ways to say something, write something, do something, experience something—whether in poetry, music, architecture, sculpture, art, prose, design, programming, speaking, loving, even to being evil and expressing wickedness. After I fell in love with my wife there seemed no end to the ways I could say "I love you,"do things for her, or imagine life together with her. When passion *claims it all* and *yields it all* for some compelling cause or experience or object or relationship, imagination frames everything one does.

The creativity of David's passion for God found expression in the form of music. Heartfelt poetry and music merged together to create awesome imagery about God—His goodness, His power, His mighty acts, His awesome holiness, and His amazing mercy. And there seems no end either to how David pours out his flood of emotions and struggles and praises and petitions in his psalms.

The biblical accounts of the role of music in David's life are as much about the imaginative power of passion as they are about the influence of music itself. As Laurin observes, "David tuned the strings of his harp on the tunes of his heart. . . . He was a musician in heart before he became one of lips and hands."[24] The apostle Paul speaks of this making melody *with* the heart—"Speaking to one another in psalms and hymns and spiritual songs, singing and making melody with your heart to the Lord; always giving thanks for all things in the name of our Lord Jesus Christ to God, even the Father" (Eph. 5:19, 20, NASB). His words suggest plucking a stringed instrument, as if one's heart were a guitar or mandolin and you made music with it. Worship, Paul suggests, has to do with the state of our heart—unbridled passion for God that overflows as music. Peterson suggests that when people realize who God is and what He does, they have no choice but to sing. "The songs are irrepressible"[25] and come bursting out. People who worship sing. We find songs everywhere in Scripture.[26] The people of God sing because worship stirs deep responses of adoration that form into rhythms and melodies of gratitude that nothing can repress.[27] "Singing is speech intensified and expanded. Song takes the natural rhythms and timbre of speech and develops its accents and intonations into music."[28] Behind all this imagination and creativity of music is passion that cannot sit still or be mediocre or be quiet or content with ordinary speech or pedestrian prose. It must dance and sing. Passion for God fills the heart with art. Accordingly, David's heart burst with purpose:

"I will sing to the Lord as long as I live; I will sing praise to my God while I have my being" (Ps. 104:33, NASB).

"My heart is steadfast, O God; I will sing, I will sing praises, even with my soul" (Ps. 108:1, NASB).

"The Lord is my strength and song, and He has become my salvation" (Ps. 118:14, NASB).

"The Lord will command His lovingkindness in the daytime; and His song will be with me in the night, a prayer to the God of my life" (Ps. 42:8, NASB).

"My lips will shout for joy when I sing praises to You; and my soul, which You have redeemed" (Ps. 71:23, NASB).

Passion in me seems to be selective. I can get passionate about a variety of things, yet other things I just can't seem to muster any energy or enthusiasm for. I know that when something has gripped my imagination, I feel it—and the passion. A fascinating force within me seems to inspire me toward creative thinking, behavior, and being. I open up to possibilities, change, and freshness—of doing things differently or better or more play-fully. I would like to think I'm passionate when it comes to God. One measure of that passion is my imagination. Indicating whether what I am into is more habit than passion, it confronts me with the reality that the vitality of my experience with God—whether expressed in prayer, wor-ship, reading Scripture, singing, witnessing, stewardship, living the Christian life, believing in His return, or tasting His grace—is a measure of my passion. If there is no imagination, I have no passion. And if I am lukewarm, something besides God grips my imagination.

A related measure of my passion is my singing. If I cannot sing or do not sing, then I must not know the joy of salvation or I am unsure about God. Does my heart make melody to God? Do spiritual songs flow through the course of my day and life, my experience with God? Has the songbook become my prayer book? What themes fill my singing? Do I sing when I am alone or only with others and at their initiative? Is music part of my personal worship experience?

I find that singing nurtures my passion for God. Also, I discover that my passion for God repeatedly summons forth heartfelt singing. Singing also nurtures my Godward imagination. And imagination, once stirred, has a subtle way of unlocking my heart when I would rather not sing. Like David, I want them both—imagination and song. Only then can I be sure that my passion for God is alive and that my worship of Him never be-comes old.

---

[1] As told by Don Campbell, *The Mozart Effect* (New York: Avon Books, 1997), pp. 60, 61.

[2] Hal A. Lingerman, *The Healing Energies of Music* (Wheaton, Ill.: Theosophical Publishing House, 1983), pp. 2, 3.

[3] C. R. Swindoll, *David: A Man of Passion and Destiny*, p. 29.

[4] C. F. Keil and F. Delitzsch, *Commentary on the Old Testament. Biblical Commentary on the Books of Samuel* (Grand Rapids: Eerdmans, 1960), vol. 2, p. 170.

[5] Lingerman, p. 14.

[6] F. W. Krummacher, *David, King of Israel* (Grand Rapids: Kregel Classics, 1994), p. 33.

[7] "The character of Saul is a marked one. There was strength and weakness combined. Gifts of talent were bestowed upon him, and had he consecrated these gifts wholly to God, he would not have dishonored himself by his own transgression. Contradictory elements were bound up in his character, and he worked at cross purposes with God. At times he revealed marked simplicity, and then was guilty of manifesting a jealous and overbearing spirit. He would be very tender and full of sympathy toward some who pleased him, as the notion came upon him, and then would be unjust and cruel toward his best friends. When brought under the influence of sacred and vocal music, he would catch the spirit of devotion, and pour forth the most impassioned expressions of lofty eloquence, in ecstasies

of praise and prayer. While under this excitement, he would give himself no rest day nor night until the reaction came. Then his strength failed, and he was exhausted. When the paroxysm of wild excitement and inordinate zeal had spent itself, he would reveal his old disposition. When his will was crossed, he was in a fury, and his words and deeds were of a character entirely dishonoring to himself, and more dishonoring to God. Good and evil were ever in collision, evil ever striving for the supremacy" (Ellen G. White Manuscript Release 926).

[8] Ellen G. White, *Patriarchs and Prophets,* p. 643.

[9] Robert D. Bergen, *1, 2 Samuel,* p. 184.

[10] "Music has no interior beacon that guarantees permanent meaning. Unlike truth, which is transcultural, absolute, and unchangeable, music can shift in meaning from place to place and time to time. Of all the art forms, music is the most flexible" (Harold M. Best, *Music Through the Eyes of Faith* [New York: HarperSanFrancisco, 1993], p. 54). "Even though music is wordless and deedless, the people making it and the contexts in which it is made are not. The more a piece of music is repeated in the same context, the more it will begin to 'mean' that context. Music is the most context friendly of all the arts. It attaches itself quickly, spongelike, to whatever surrounds it" (*ibid.*). On the other hand, the "Word of God is not context absorbing; it is context disturbing. It does not change with the context. Rather, the context must change because of its presence" (*ibid.,* p. 55).

[11] Adapted from Campbell, pp. 64-78.

[12] Campbell, p. 179.

[13] White, *Patriarchs and Prophets,* pp. 36, 37.

[14] ———, *The Story of Redemption* (Washington, D.C.: Review and Herald Pub. Assn., 1947), p. 25.

[15] ———, *The Desire of Ages,* p. 73.

[16] Anne Lamott, *Traveling Mercies: Some Thoughts on Faith* (New York: Pantheon Books, 1999), pp. 44-51.

[17] Adapted from Philip Yancey, *What's So Amazing About Grace?* (Grand Rapids: Zondervan Publishing House, 1997), pp. 281, 282.

[18] Keith Kaynor, *When God Chooses: The Life of David,* p. 31.

[19] *Ibid.*

[20] White, *Patriarchs and Prophets,* p. 637.

[21] *Ibid.,* p. 642.

[22] Roddy Braun, *1 Chronicles, Word Biblical Commentary* (Waco, Tex.: Word Books, Publisher, 1986), vol. 14, p. 246.

[23] Swindoll, p. 32.

[24] Roy L. Laurin, *Designed for Conquest* (Grand Rapids: Kregel Publications, 1990), p. 71.

[25] Eugene H. Peterson, *Reversed Thunder: The Revelation of John and the Praying Imagination* (New York: HarperSanFrancisco, 1991), p. 66.

[26] Music fills heaven (Rev. 4; 5); the 144,000 sing a new song; the redeemed who come through tribulation sing the Song of Moses and the Lamb (Rev. 15); Moses sings. Miriam sings. Deborah sings. David sings. Mary sings. Angels sing. Jesus and His disciples sing. Paul and Silas sing. God Himself sings.

[27] Peterson, p. 68.

[28] *Ibid.,* p. 66.

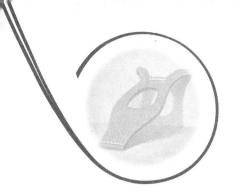

4

LET ME OUT OF HERE!

I Samuel 17:12-15

When the Luray, Virginia, Seventh-day Adventist Church held a twenty-fifth-anniversary celebration commemorating its move from rented quarters to a brand-new building, I had the privilege of preaching the Sabbath morning message. Luray was the church district I started out in as a ministerial intern after graduating from Southern Adventist University. The 18 months that Kathie and I spent with the Luray people—and those from the Stanley congregation just eight miles south—were unforgettably precious and remarkably formative to me as a young intern. They are special people there. Some who are now sleeping in Jesus linger well in my memory, and their influence often tugs at my heart still today after so many years. Needless to say, returning for the anniversary brought back many fond memories and not a few tears.

One thing I was not prepared for was the awe-inspiring reminder of just how magnificent the countryside around Luray is. "I could take a steady diet of this!" I kept saying to myself as I traveled along Virginia's scenic U.S. 211, which runs between Warrenton and Luray. Its meandering road ascends the glorious Blue Ridge Mountains, then drops down into the stunning Shenandoah Valley on the other side. As you crest the Blue Ridge Mountains you cross over the famous Skyline Drive—a winding road that runs along the ridge of this portion of Appalachia. I had forgotten just how lovely it all was. Winding, often narrow roads offered vistas of spectacular landscape at nearly every turn. Everywhere we saw rolling hillsides, quiet meadows, and grazing cattle along with an occasional deer. It was a land of incredible sunsets and sunrises, waterfalls, rippling streams, magnificent trees, stone rows, split-rail fences, and autumn colors. The region contained two national forests, hanging wisps of mist, abundant wildlife, quaint historic towns, and cool nights. "Yes, I could live here again. Easily. Just give me a chance!"

That's why so many in the Luray area work in Washington, D.C., or northern Virginia (some 80 or so miles northeast), but live in Luray. Quite a few from our Luray congregation commuted back then, too. I remember some who made the daily drive that took two-plus hours each way. Others had a room they rented or a van they slept in during the week, returning only on the weekend. One or two had a cot in their offices. I used to think it odd and an inconvenient hassle. So much time away from home and on the road seemed senseless and inefficient to me. Why commute? Why not live closer to your work? Why not get a job nearby? Wouldn't it be better for family life and one's own well-being? You'd be around so you could do more in the church, too!

This Pennsylvania boy who grew up in similar Appalachia country should have known the answer. Efficiency and proximity are not everything. Nor is time, or the big city, or even one's work. Commuting often expresses a conscious choice to maintain a level of personal simplicity and solitude in the midst of an otherwise complicated and congested world of work and life. Why uproot life for work? Just go and do your work, then return home to life. We long for quiet and privacy. A home tucked far enough away from the hassles of work and life in the big city can be a haven for personal and spiritual sanity. Many think it's worth the commute.

David was a commuter![1] Scripture tells us that when he came to the palace as Saul's personal music therapist, he didn't get an apartment and stay. "David went back and forth from Saul to tend his father's flock at Bethlehem" (1 Sam. 17:15, NASB). It's intriguing that after being anointed as Israel's next king, David kept on tending his flocks (1 Sam. 16:19). And he returned to the sheep after becoming Saul's personal musician (1 Sam. 17:15). It tells us something about David and his interests and priorities—where his heart and mind really were. At first he didn't have much choice except to rejoin his sheep. But once he became part of Saul's court, it was a different story.

Saul had his court in Gibeah about four miles north of Jerusalem, while David lived in Bethlehem approximately five miles south of Jerusalem (1 Sam. 10:26; 15:34; 22:6; 23:19). It was no easy commute following the winding road up and down that rugged countryside on foot. David regularly traveled the nine-plus miles back and forth from Saul's palace to the hills where he tended his father's sheep. The Hebrew literally reads "he was going and returning." The verb forms are participial, pointing to continuous action. There's more here, though, than just the idea of physical motion or movement. Something significant was taking place in David's mind and heart. He was going to Saul, but returning to the sheep. The Hebrew word for "return" is *shûb,* and Scripture often uses it to imply a coming back to where one once was. Old Testament writers employed the word in the context of returning to God (in the sense of repentance), or turning away from evil (in the sense of renouncing and disowning sin).

David didn't need to commute to work in Saul's court. He could have stayed in Gibeah and lived in the royal residence. Earlier in the story we read that "Saul loved him greatly, and he became his armor bearer. Saul sent to Jesse, saying, 'Let David now stand before me, for he has found favor in my sight'" (1 Sam. 16:21, 22, NASB). The Hebrew word for "stand" is *'âmad,* and often means "to remain standing, continue, endure, or abide." The New International Version catches Saul's point well: "Allow David to remain in my service, for I am pleased with him" (verse 22). In other words, Saul wanted to keep David there instead of having him coming and going. The shepherd-musician was not a permanent fixture in Saul's court. Evidently he would show up when the king needed his soothing music, but once he accomplished his task, the young man quietly slipped away to the hills to tend his father's sheep. One gets the feeling that all this travel back and forth was David's choice, not Saul's or Jesse's. There was something significant that David kept returning to—something more than just caring for his father's sheep.[2]

David chose to commute because he desired to maintain a level of personal simplicity and solitude in the midst of an otherwise complicated assignment as musician in Saul's troubled court. He longed for the quiet and privacy of the outdoors. The shepherd-musician wanted to think, pray, and sing without distraction. The fields with his father's sheep were tucked far enough away from the hassles and confusion of his new work to offer a haven for his personal and spiritual sanity. It was worth the commute.

Unforgettable Contrasts

When I visited the Ukraine for the first time to hold a series of evangelistic meetings, the stark contrasts between my own life and that of the Ukrainian people struck me greatly. Not only did I encounter a mind-boggling disparity between our standards of living (it was as if I had stepped back 50 years in time into a world that had stood still while mine had moved on), but I found heartrending differences between our experiences with life itself. Here were people who hadn't received a paycheck in months, whose water and/or electricity would be turned off unexpectedly each day, and whose roads were filled with deep potholes and flooded with water running out from deteriorating buildings or broken watermains. Shops and markets were largely empty of goods. Their money inflated almost daily. Many a night during those meetings I looked into a sea of tired, pain-filled faces and heard heartrending stories that reached far beyond material things. Struggling with the absence of God in their life and world, they had troubled consciences and lives filled with the pain of self-inflicted wounds as well as the incredible dysfunction that Communism had left in its wake. I found minds struggling with the futility of the material to really satisfy the soul. A sense of despair and helplessness from not being able to really change the quality of their life or to experience real peace and find hope for the future continually wore them down. In many ways it was a relief for me to return to the United States after living with the Ukrainian people in their homes for more than seven weeks. The moment my KLM flight lifted from the Kiev runway, I heaved a sigh. I was leaving behind all the inconvenience and pain they experienced. Back at home, though, I could not get those contrasts out of my mind. They were unforgettable. Though I would return to the Ukraine several more times, deep inside I never wanted to "really" experience what the Ukrainian people were going through. A few weeks here or there was quite enough—and never like the real thing. Unlike me, they were trapped.

That's how David felt when he encountered the stark contrasts between his life in the hills of Bethlehem and that in Saul's court—but from the opposite direction than my experience. David was just a backwoods shepherd lad who landed his prestigious job as the king's private music therapist. Unlike me, he entered a world of affluence and distinction, opportunity and ease. The palace was where Israel's shakers and movers gathered. "What luck!" one might have been tempted to say. The contrast, though, between David's humble shepherd life and that in the court was unforgettably painful. Like my example, the contrasts went far beyond the material—they involved the spiritual and moral as well. When David saw the kind of things that he found in Saul's court, commuting became his key to moral and spiritual sanity.

Entering Saul's court, David essentially stepped into a secular environment in which moral values and spiritual principles did not serve as guiding norms in personal life, thought, or leadership. Questionable things took place behind those royal walls and in the hearts and lives of those dwelling there. His eyes now opened, he lost some of his innocence as he saw the emptiness of affluence, power, and life lived just for the temporal. Remember, Saul wasn't all that interested in God, and he didn't consider obedience that important. If you are not all that involved with God, you won't be all that concerned about doing His will. Saul was interested only in himself: what the people thought, the perks that went with being king, and living life now.

Furthermore, he was a troubled man. Moody, Saul struggled with a tormenting spirit that included depression, outbursts of anger, and degrading fits of insanity. Anyone who has lived in a home with any degree of dysfunction—one in which a member of the family is emotionally or mentally unstable or perpetually unhappy—knows that it is an unhealthy environment that literally wears people down emotionally. It can drain your passion for anything.

Thus, "when his services were not required at the court of Saul, David returned to his flocks among the hills and continued to maintain his simplicity of spirit and demeanor. Whenever it was necessary, he was recalled to minister before the king, to soothe the mind of the troubled monarch till the evil spirit should depart from him. But although Saul expressed delight in David and his music, the young shepherd went from the king's house to the fields and hills of his pasture with a sense of relief and gladness."[3] He commuted for a reason.

Ellen White also tells how in Saul's court David found "new themes for thought. He had . . . seen the responsibilities of royalty. He had discovered some of the temptations that beset the soul of Saul and had penetrated some of the mysteries in the character and dealings of Israel's first king. He had seen the glory of royalty shadowed with a dark cloud of sorrow, and he knew that the household of Saul, in their private life, were far from happy. All these things served to bring troubled thoughts to him who had been anointed to be king over Israel. . . . While he was absorbed in deep meditation, and harassed by thoughts of anxiety, he turned to his harp, and called forth strains that elevated his mind to the Author of every good, and the dark clouds that seemed to shadow the horizon of the future were dispelled."[4]

As David gained a clear view of the king and life in the palace, he wanted to get away more and more. He sensed how life in the court depleted his passion for God. But what did he experience in the field while tending his father's flocks that kept drawing him back? We've gotten a feel for what David encountered in Saul's court, but what did he find in the pasturelands around Bethlehem?

Psalm 19 offers a substantial clue. You will remember that David's psalms arose out of both his life experiences and God's dealings with his heart. They portray the characteristics and habits of his heart. His psalms not only allow a glimpse into his view of God; they offer windows to his inner self as well—his thoughts, feelings, fears, questions, resolve. As a shepherd, David was an outdoorsman who spent many hours—literally day and night—absorbing the beauty and mysteries of nature. Before him spread a landscape of rich and varied beauty—the overarching heavens, the thunderstorms, and awe-inspiring sunrises. Beyond all this incredible beauty was God. Nature provides one of the most tangible links with Him, something David instinctively grasped. David could not see the Creator, but His works in nature revealed His ways. "As he contemplated the perfections of his Creator, clearer conceptions of God opened before his soul."[5] In the pasturelands and hills

David was finding God and observing His ways.

Written during his youthful years, Psalm 19 reflects the kind of tension David would likely have experienced during his yo-yo life of shepherd and royal musician. It begins majestically with the eloquence of nature, halfway through it moves powerfully to the clarity of Scripture, and then it concludes unexpectedly with a profound sense of personal vulnerability, confession, and prayer. When we read Psalm 19 we need to imagine someone meditating on the ways God makes His presence known (through nature and Scripture) and what kind of heart could truly commune with Him:

"The heavens are telling of the glory of God; and their expanse is declaring the work of His hands.

"Day to day pours forth speech, and night to night reveals knowledge. There is no speech, nor are there words; their voice is not heard.

"Their line has gone out through all the earth, and their utterances to the end of the world. In them He has placed a tent for the sun,

"Which is as a bridegroom coming out of his chamber; it rejoices as a strong man to run his course.

"Its rising is from one end of the heavens, and its circuit to the other end of them; and there is nothing hidden from its heat.

"The law of the Lord is perfect, restoring the soul; the testimony of the Lord is sure, making wise the simple.

"The precepts of the Lord are right, rejoicing the heart; the commandment of the Lord is pure, enlightening the eyes.

"The fear of the Lord is clean, enduring forever; the judgments of the Lord are true; they are righteous altogether.

"They are more desirable than gold, yes, than much fine gold; sweeter also than honey and the drippings of the honeycomb.

"Moreover, by them Your servant is warned; in keeping them there is great reward. Who can discern his errors? Acquit me of hidden faults.

"Also keep back Your servant from presumptuous sins; let them not rule over me; then I shall be blameless, and I shall be acquitted of great transgression.

"Let the words of my mouth and the meditation of my heart be acceptable in Your sight, O Lord, my rock and my Redeemer" (Ps. 19, NASB).

Inevitable Choices

The contrasts David confronted as both shepherd and royal musician lay between life as seen from the perspective of Saul's secular court and life in relation to the living God of heaven as evidenced in the wonders of nature and the truths of Scripture. No one can keep up the kind of seesaw and schizophrenic routine David experienced without it causing them to stop and consider the differences in the respective lifestyles, values, and priorities. Such contrasts and tensions provide an unparalleled opportunity for moral and spiritual reflection. They lead ultimately toward moral and spiritual choice. In fact, they force the issue. At some point, one *must* choose. Moral and spiritual equilibrium does not allow one to halt between two opinions indefinitely. Psalm 19 reflects the kind of valuation and choice that David faced. Deeply aware of God's presence in nature and Scripture, he affirmed that he wanted no part of the dysfunction and emptiness he saw in the royal court. What the world there promised to offer did not attract him at all. He saw the reality of it all—its attitudes, lifestyle, fears, brokenness, folly, ignorance, unhappiness, and emptiness.

"What really restores one's spirit to full vigor and vitality?" he asked himself. "Is it found in life in the royal court? No! It is found in the law of the Lord (see verse 7).

"What really provides the wisdom that keeps life from culminating in the disasters of folly (making wise the simple)? Is it found in the royal court? No! It is found in the testimony of the Lord (see verse 7).

"What creates that rejoicing rooted in a life of uprightness before God (rejoicing the heart)? It is the precepts of the Lord (see verse 8).

"What really reveals the dimensions of truth and reality in human existence (enlightening the eyes)? The commandments of the Lord (see verse 8).

"What really endures forever? What is life's only permanent foundation? The fear of the Lord (see verse 9). This stuff in the court isn't where it's at.

"And what about the extravagant wealth and delectable food that comes with the privileged status and power of court life? Do they really satisfy the soul? Do they have any ultimate value? No! Even fine gold is less desirable than God's Word, *Torah* (see verse 10). Only the Word of

God can warn of evil and potential dangers. Obeying it leads to great personal reward (see verse 11)."[6]

Thus David yearned to be different than the secular or spiritually empty world around him. Desiring God in his heart, he wanted to obey God. Yet he realized his own vulnerability—how the subtle influences of court life could attach themselves to him and lead him to both hidden faults and presumptuous sins. How he could become jaded and just as much a part of the court as anyone else. So he whispered to God, "Who can discern his errors? Acquit me of hidden faults. Also keep back Your servant from presumptuous sins; let them not rule over me; then I shall be blameless, and I shall be acquitted of great transgression. Let the words of my mouth and the meditation of my heart be acceptable in Your sight, O Lord, my rock and my Redeemer" (verses 12-14, NASB).

Struggling with the fickleness of his own heart, David claims God's transforming presence. He wanted passion for God over passion for the royal court.

Passion Renews Itself

In his book *Restoring Your Spiritual Passion* Gordon MacDonald notes: "Yesterday's spiritual passion cannot be today's inner energy. Passion quickly dissipates; it must be restored. Like the manna God gave the Israelites in the desert, spiritual passion spoils quickly. As Moses and his people had to collect manna daily, so must we restore spiritual passion regularly. We would be wise to know how it so quickly disappears and what we can do when that happens."[7]

David understood this truth about passion for God. Because it dissipates quickly, it must be renewed, and regularly. He sensed, too, that both the bald-faced and the subtle influences of Saul's court could very well deplete his passion for God and that he needed life in the field to sustain it. His perhaps almost daily commute was absolutely essential to preserving his passion for God. Thus David disciplined himself to regularly step apart and commune with God in the field in order to regain perspective—and to renew his spiritual passion.

Passion renews itself! By nature it is self-renewing. There is something absorbing about passion. When we have passion we get blinders on our eyes and fix our focus on whatever stirs that passion. People with passion find conscious ways to design more of what they love into their everyday existence. As one man said: "Knowing what I am passionate about has put real power in my hands. It's as though I'm walking around holding a plug, seeking outlets where I can connect to it and express more." Passion seeks more. And it is also the ultimate time-management tool.[8] When you're doing what you love, who cares about time? As you spend time with someone you love, or listening to a great piece of music, or experiencing something you really enjoy—time just flies by, and things get done faster than when you are doing only the things you need to do. Living by your passion keeps your passion stirred.

David's commute, then, was not just the *practical* thing to do, or something he *had* to do. It was something he *wanted* to do because he already had passion for God and sought to keep it overflowing. His passion for God led him to the field and served as his "time-management" tool. He was allowing what was most important to him—the One he loved the most and desired to be with the most—to determine his schedule, his whereabouts, and the kind of influence that would dominate his imagination.

I find in David's routine commute a call to a new level of intimacy with God. A summons to deepened devotional life—to the spiritual disciplines that both nurture and renew our passion for God: prayer; reading Scripture; singing hymns, spiritual songs, and making melody in our hearts to God; and quiet moments of meditation, self-examination, and moral resolve. My calendar broadcasts my passion.

If passion is the ultimate time-management tool, how am I spending my time? What does my day or week look like? Is it spent mostly in the royal court or at least proportionately in the field? Is it with the world or with God? Am I a commuter? Or have I only gone out into the world? Am I venturing out into my family, work, ministry, and culture, and never returning (or rarely returning) to restore my soul and hold on to my spiritual roots—to be with God? My answers to these questions reveal whether or not I have passion for God or passion for something else.

Passion renews itself. If I am not actively and consciously and joyfully renewing my passion for God—not out of duty or because I'm afraid I'll lose it—then passion must not have yet claimed all my heart. I will spend my time and the energies of my heart where my passion leads. It's a given.

Because passion is a barometer, if mine leads me toward God, then He is my passion. As long as I am actively and regularly renewing my passion for Him, then I can trust that this passion I have is more real than not. When I live on the basis of my passion, I can be sure it is my passion.

My wife is a commuter. Kathie has a nearly two-mile walk with her Bible down the dirt road we live on to a place that she has made for herself between open fields. She'll make that journey rain or shine, bone-chilling cold or soggy heat, in the morning or at midnight—just to be with God and pour out her heart to Him. A mother of four sons and a minister's wife who manages her own business, she interacts daily with people from all walks of life and belief. And she's a prayer warrior for people for whom God has placed a burden on her heart—many times not knowing why. Thus she commutes to keep perspective and equilibrium. She commutes because sometimes there is no one really to talk to but God. She commutes because the people in her life matter. She commutes because a burden for someone or something—and she can't figure out why—is churning in her heart. And she commutes because her passion needs restoring. I sensed a newness in her life when she first began her ritual. Through the years I have watched her spiritual fervor deepen, her passion for God strengthen. And I have seen God at work both in her life and in the lives of those for whom she prays—even mine—because she commutes.

Every once in a while I journey out to those fields with Kathie. She'll point toward a particular place in the sky and with watery eyes exclaim, "There's God's throne. I tug on His robe that hangs down through the sky . . . right there!" I look up and try to imagine. All I see is sky. No throne. No hem of a robe. No God. Just sky or sometimes clouds. But for Kathie, God is there. The robe she tugs on is real. Each time she comes to this sacred meeting place on the edge of an ordinary field—she renews her passion for God. She comes because of her passion for God, then leaves with even more. The invisible God really is there.

Yancey observes that in the Bible "the greatest distinction between human beings is not based on race, intelligence, income, or talent. It is a distinction based on correspondence with the unseen world."[9] As Paul writes, "the unspiritual man simply cannot accept the matters which the Spirit deals with—they just don't make sense to him, for, after all, you must be spiritual to see spiritual things. The spiritual man, on the other hand, has an insight into the meaning of everything" (1 Cor. 2:14-16, Phillips). "Although you have not seen him, you love him; and even though you do not see him now, you believe in him and rejoice with an indescribable and glorious joy," Peter declares (1 Peter 1:8, NRSV). "We walk by faith, not by sight" (2 Cor. 5:7). And faith "means being certain of things we cannot see" (Heb. 11:1, Phillips). A pathway leads into the unseen world—to God. People with passion have found it and follow it incessantly. They become who they are by relating to God—and in the process they become passionate about God.

Someone once snapped off the antenna on my car, leaving me with absolutely no radio reception except the local FM station that broadcasts from the village near where I live. For some reason I just kept driving—for years, in fact—never getting it fixed. I couldn't get the news station I wanted to listen to. Nor could I pick up anything from beyond the broadcast radius of that local FM station. Obviously, being able to listen to my radio wasn't all that important to me. If I had been passionate about it, I would have immediately fixed it. After all, antennas aren't that expensive or difficult to install. Some of us are like that. We're driving through life with a broken antenna. All we can get is the local station called the world. If we would only put up the antenna, we could reach beyond our immediate world. Then we would hear God speaking to our soul and would receive what we need in order to either ignite or renew our passion for Him. The spiritual disciplines of my commute are like putting up my antenna. As with David, it not only makes a difference; it happens because we're different. Passion renews itself.

------

[1] Ralph W. Klein, *1 Samuel, Word Biblical Commentary,* vol. 10, p. 177.

[2] Some have suggested that because Saul was on military maneuvers he did not need David and the young shepherd had returned home for a while, or because three of David's brothers were serving Saul as soldiers his father required his help with the flocks. While these are possibilities, they do not fully express the persistent cycle that the participial forms of "going and returning" suggest, or why the narrator thinks it is important for us to see David as still tending sheep when Samuel had anointed him Israel's next king. See Joyce Baldwin, *1 and 2 Samuel: Introduction and Commentary* (Downers Grove, Ill.: Inter-Varsity Press, 1988), p. 126; Klein, p. 177.

[3] Ellen G. White, *Patriarchs and Prophets,* p. 643.

[4] *Ibid.,* p. 644.

[5] *Ibid.,* p. 642.

[6] Adapted from Peter Craigie, *Psalms 1-50, Word Biblical Commentary,* vol. 19, pp. 181, 182.

[7] Gordon MacDonald, *Restoring Your Spiritual Passion*, p. 37.
[8] Marcia Wieder, *Doing Less and Having More*, pp. 97, 192, 193.
[9] Philip Yancey, *Reaching for the Invisible God*, p. 106.

5

FRIENDLY FIRE

I Samuel 17:12-30

The vision of two armies drawing up against each other in battle array—shouting war cries—has got to be one of the most gripping scenes that one could ever imagine. The sense that at any moment two armed forces would rush toward each other and clash in the frenzied commotion of brutal hand-to-hand combat—in which soldiers would be impaled, maimed, trampled, and die in agony and in which history would turn on the outcome—would undoubtedly be both exciting and frightening at the same time.

I'm trying to imagine what must have gone through David's mind as he came over the top of the hill and saw the quickly forming lines of Israelite and Philistine soldiers in the Valley of Elah. Scripture tells us that David arrived in camp just as the two armies rushed to confront each other: "He came to the circle of the camp while the army was going out in battle array shouting the war cry. Israel and the Philistines drew up in battle array, army against army" (1 Sam. 17:20, 21, NASB). Earlier in the story we learn that "the Philistines stood on the mountain on one side while Israel stood on the mountain on the other side, with the valley between them" (verse 3, NASB). I wonder what went through David's mind. Did he stand and stare open-mouthed as he sized up the spectacular scene? No doubt he was excited and wanted to watch, to get closer, to see what was going to happen. Any young person would. For that matter, any adult would too. In fact, David was so eager to see the battle and find out more about it, that he left the provisions he had brought for his brothers and literally ran to the front line where his brothers faced off with the enemy (verse 22).

Picture the moment! The early-morning sunlight glittered off weapons as troops moved into position. The Elah Valley is a mile-wide depression that runs northwest along the lower hill country some 17 miles southwest of Jerusalem. The Philistines drew up on the west side of the valley near a place called Ephes-dammim (verse 1). It was a name with an ominous meaning—"the boundary of bloods," likely receiving its name because on more than one occasion it had been the scene of fierce border forays between the Israelites and their restless warlike neighbors.[1] Saul took up position on the eastern side of the valley. Each side stationed itself on the sloping hillsides that formed the valley. Thus each army had high ground, enlisting gravity to add momentum to their arrows, spears, and projectiles if the enemy should charge. Both armies looked down on a central arena consisting of a comparatively level strip of land through which a small watercourse flowed during the rainy season.

While it was a half mile or so up the slope on either side, some have suggested that the two armies may have been located at a point where the valley narrowed so that they were only about 300 yards apart.[2] Can you imagine facing your enemy just three football fields away? That's close enough to engage at a moment's notice. Each side could see the intimidating forest of spears and shields held by the enemy's solid front line, hear the rattle of the sword, and perhaps even make out expressions on faces. Thus soldiers from each side hurled insults at one another and shouted the war cry. Intimidation was the name of the game! Get close, but don't engage. Unnerve the enemy. Frighten them out of their wits. And in the process, pump yourself up. That was the whole purpose of the war cry—intimidation, psyching oneself up, and creating a mob mentality that would numb your mind for battle if the order came to charge.

What David encountered became a 40-day routine (verse 16). Forty mornings the two armies had formed solid lines along the valley across from each other. During the day they challenged each other—marching around, shouting war cries, hurling insults, strutting their stuff. Then at night they would return to their tents. Both armies, as they tried to psych themselves up and unnerve the enemy, had reason to be nervous. Saul had badly beaten the Philistines at Michmash (1 Sam. 13:23–14:23). So they weren't about to rush into another all-out confrontation until things were just right. The Israelites, on the other hand, didn't have the kind of weapons the Philistines had. Nor did they have the same quality of training.

Goliath was part of the daily ritual. Scripture tells us that every day—twice a day, for 40 days—the huge heavily armed Philistine brute would emerge from the solid line of Philistine soldiers and descend to the valley floor (1 Sam. 17:16). He would approach close enough to be clearly seen by Israel's front lines. Then he would strut his stuff and challenge the children of Israel to send someone to fight: "Do you need a whole army to settle this? Choose someone to fight for you, and I will represent the Philistines. We will settle this dispute in single combat! If your man is able to kill me, then we will be your slaves. But if I kill him, you will be our slaves! I defy the armies of Israel! Send me a man who will fight with me!" (verses 8-10, NLT).

Goliath's appearance was impressive, and his words were clear, crisp, foreboding. The results were devastating. "When Saul and all Israel heard those words of the Philistine, they were dismayed, and greatly afraid" (verse 11). "When all the men of Israel saw the man, they fled from him and were greatly afraid" (verse 24, NASB). Goliath was skilled in the art of boasting. The mind game was working well.

For 40 days the Israelites and Philistines taunted each other. After they had shouted themselves hoarse and the whole game would get kind of old, Goliath would appear. In an instant the front lines on the Israelite army would melt away (verse 24). The Philistines would laugh and hoot, and the spirits of the Israelites would drop one notch lower. None dared to meet Goliath alone in combat to resolve the issue between the two armies. The Goliath routine was the last thing they experienced at the end of the day before they returned to their tents.

Little Brothers, Big Brothers

David takes it all in. At first he's caught up in the excitement. But then Goliath appears with his blasphemous boasts and in-your-face challenge. As the lowest line of soldiers on the hill retreat out of the giant's reach,

David is stunned, unable to believe it. Would no one respond? Surely, in a moment, someone would step forth to silence the burly bigmouth. But no one did. Surprisingly, big brother Eliab did not say a thing. And neither did Abinadab and Shammah. I can hear David thinking to himself about now, *Why doesn't Eliab do something? Or Abinadab? Or Shammah? They've been out here with Saul's army all this time and have heard Goliath's challenge and mockery. Why don't they do something?* (see verse 13). Perhaps in family gatherings he had listened to his enlisted brothers tell tales of training, valor, and bravado. Likely they had announced all the things they were going to do to those uncirumcised Philistines. How they would rid the land of them. But now the brothers said nothing. As the moments passed, David overheard some of the men around him talking: "'Have you seen the giant?' the men were asking. 'He comes out each day to challenge Israel. And have you heard about the huge reward the king has offered to anyone who kills him? The king will give him one of his daughters for a wife, and his whole family will be exempted from paying taxes!'" (verse 25, NLT).

His interest aroused, David spoke with some others standing there to verify the report. "What will a man get for killing this Philistine and putting an end to his abuse of Israel?" he asked (verse 26, NLT). "Who is this pagan Philistine anyway, that he is allowed to defy the armies of the living God?" (verse 26, NLT).

"What you have been hearing is true," they replied (verse 27, NLT). "That is the reward for killing the giant" (verse 27, NLT). "The king will enrich the man who kills him and will give him his daughter and make his father's house free in Israel."

That's when Eliab lost it—"When David's oldest brother, Eliab, heard David talking to the men, he was angry. 'What are you doing around here anyway?' he demanded. 'What about those few sheep you're supposed to be taking care of? I know about your pride and dishonesty. You just want to see the battle!'" (verse 28, NLT). I can see his sneering face and fiery eyes. Obviously, David was not able altogether to conceal from those who stood near him the feelings that were in his mind. The impetuosity with which he added the question "Who is this uncircumcised Philistine, that he should defy the armies of the living God?" fully revealed his inmost thoughts.[3] Then as he began asking questions about Saul's generous incentives, he showed himself not a little interested.[4] In other words, he intended to do something about it if no one else was—and in the process, collect the reward.

Patriarchs and Prophets tells us that when Eliab heard David's comments, he instantly recognized what was going through his younger brother's mind. "Even as a shepherd, David had manifested daring, courage, and strength rarely witnessed; and the mysterious visit of Samuel to their father's house, and his silent departure, had awakened in the minds of the brothers suspicions of the real object of his visit."[5] Eliab had likely heard David tell stories about how he killed a bear and a lion and had other such daring escapades. It's hard for an older brother to handle someone like David—courageous, musical, aggressive, spiritual, a good worker, good-looking, strong, and who's landed a prestigious job in the palace. Everything is here for classic sibling rivalry and jealousy. Brueggemann notes that Eliab's anger is not directed against either the Israelites or Philistines. "No, he is angry with little David. Well, of course. Little brothers bother big brothers, especially if big brothers are pretending to be mighty men of valor—who are immobilized in fear and cannot fight. David's presence immediately exposes Eliab as a coward, and all the men with him."[6] Gordon puts it bluntly: "Eliab's anger is the anger of a man who feels small because of the Israelite army's inability to deal with Goliath, and he particularly resents looking small in the eyes of his young brother."[7] David's brothers were the ones who had enlisted, following Saul off to war (verse 13). But these so-called warriors and big talkers at home were now wimps, cowards, and out of touch with God. When it came right down to it, they didn't have the right stuff.

So what did Eliab do? As is the case whenever someone feels embarrassed, ineffective, a failure, or empty, he diverted attention away from himself and his weakness, away from his fear and his emptiness, to David's problems. He said everything that he could think of to discourage and belittle his brother and get the spotlight off himself. And he does this by raising questions about David's motives: "Look, David, why have you really showed up here?" Then Eliab asks a question designed to humiliate David. "Hey, David, where did you leave that handful of sheep?" Finally he gets downright ugly: "I know your insolence and the wickedness of your heart. You just came here for the excitement. You just wanted to see the battle." Thus Eliab questions David's motives, implies he's irresponsible, insults him, and demeans his work as a mere shepherd. "David, you don't belong here. Go home!" The reader, though, knows that all the charges are empty and inappropriate. David came because his father had asked him to: "Take this half-bushel of roasted grain and these ten loaves of bread to your brothers. And give these ten cuts of cheese to their captain. See how your brothers are getting along, and bring me back a letter from them" (verses 17, 18, NLT).

Eliab claimed he knew all about the evil in David's heart, but he didn't. Had he really understood his brother's heart, he would have recognized that David was a man after the heart of God.[8] He obviously diagnosed David's heart exactly the opposite of what God had. By calling his brother proud (verse 28), Eliab revealed his own heart. Liars think that most others are liars just as thieves assume everyone else is a thief or proud people see their own arrogance in others and hate them for it. Isn't it interesting how we can so easily and readily project our own guilt into somebody else's life? In his classic *My Utmost for His Highest* Oswald Chambers has a reading titled "The Uncritical Temper" based on the words of Jesus, "Judge not, that ye be not judged" (Matt. 7:1). "The effect of criticism is a dividing up of the powers of the one criticized; the Holy Ghost is the only One in the true position to criticize, He alone is able to show what is wrong without hurting and wounding. It is impossible to enter into communion with God when you are in a critical temper. . . . If I see the mote in your eye, it means I have a beam in my own. Every wrong thing that I see in you, God locates in me. . . . I have never met the man I could despair of after discerning what lies in me apart from the grace of God."[9]

I wonder how much like Eliab we are—competitive in spirit, critical by nature. Rather than delighting in the success and effectiveness of others, we explain it away or try to tear it down. In the process, our own passion subsides as we spend more and more time jealously looking sideways at the road others are taking rather than focusing on the path God has paved for us.[10] The tendency to emphasize the negative in every situation, or to find character faults prevents us from generating the positive energy we need to do the work to which God calls us.[11] Both competitive and critical spirits rendered Eliab powerless and passionless. The incident reminds us that we dare not question the motives of others. Because we cannot read another person's heart we need to be careful that we do not project into someone else's words or actions our own motives and attitudes.

In effect, Eliab was for David what MacDonald calls a very draining person—someone who saps our spiritual passion.[12] The people around us both give and take passion from us. Eliab was a taker.

Friendly Fire and Choosing Our Battles

One of the great literary pieces that came out of the Vietnam War was a book called *Friendly Fire*.[13] It detailed the events surrounding the death of Michael Eugene Mullen, a young American soldier, during a jungle fire-fight, and the failure of the Defense Department to account for what had actually taken place. Only after the dead soldier's persistent parents demanded full disclosure did it become clear that Mullen had not lost his life to the enemy but to misdirected artillery fire from American guns. The military term for such an accident is *friendly fire*. He had been killed by his fellow soldiers. "Friendly fire? *Friendly fire?*" Mullen's mother repeated incredulously when an Army spokesman first broke the news in her kitchen. "*Not* the enemy! @&#!*%# you! You couldn't even give him the . . . decency of being killed by the enemy!" she glared.[14]

"Friendly fire" in Vietnam came from more than misdirected artillery rounds or stray bullets in the confusion of jungle firefights. It also consisted of biased news reports of battle situations, impassioned antiwar demonstrations back home, racial tensions, and petty personal differences among the soldiers in the field as well as the wrenching struggle over the moral issues of the war that often surfaced among them. And each time "friendly fire" left American soldiers wounded in spirit and created an environment from which some never came home again. Popular movie and television programming like *Platoon* and *Tour of Duty* and a myriad of books and talk shows have highlighted the picture of soldiers fighting a war while often preoccupied with hurts that kept them from concentrating on the real enemy. Surrounding the battle with the Viet Cong were many little battles with fellow Americans at home and in the foxholes that sapped their spirit and drained their passion.

Unfortunately, "friendly fire" is not unusual among those who would have passion for God. You've experienced it. "Friendly guns"—fellow church members, parents, children, a spouse, a sibling, colleagues at work, employees or leaders—have fired on you. Wherever it comes from, "friendly fire" can destroy our spiritual passion.

David knew the sting of disapproval and jealousy by his brothers—"friendly fire." He experienced what many go through when they take a position or demonstrate faith or prove themselves to be better in some way. They get flak. People around them say and do things that sap passion for God. It often comes from members of their own family or church or from colleagues in the workplace—from those who are near and dear and who ought to know better. No one can encourage or discourage us like family. The views of our family members toward us are very convincing. As MacDonald suggests, the person who sets out to serve God must understand that a kind of guerrilla warfare rages around them. All too often passion for God gets dissipated by surrounding battles, battles that we have never taken time to adequately understand. The enemies of passion are so well camouflaged that they are almost impossible to ferret out, much less destroy. Keeping our spiritual passion means understanding the kinds of spiritual battles that will deny us the energy we need.[15] Coming to grips with "friendly fire" is part of it.

Given Eliab's outburst, the average person would have rolled up their sleeves and used all their energy to punch the brother's lights out. And if they couldn't do that, they'd likely talk big and spew out some of their own verbal venom in retaliation. There would be some kind of fight for sure. In the process, the real enemy, Goliath, would still be haranguing his heart out. But David is bigger than that. He basically ignores his big brother's tongue-lashing, as if to say, "Hey, all I did was ask a question." Then David just turns away. "A gentle answer turns away wrath, but a harsh word stirs up anger" (Prov. 15:1, NIV). Scrapping with his brother was not what David had in mind. He was concerned about Goliath and didn't want to get sidetracked. Somehow, perhaps by long experience with his brothers, David knew that the people around him either nurtured or drained his passion for God. A current of passion would be moving in one direction or another, either toward him or away from him. He wasn't about to get into the kind of scrap that would deplete his passion. As Swindoll observes, David knew who to fight and who to avoid. "We need to choose our battles wisely," he comments. "If you don't watch it, all of your battles will be fought among fellow members of the family of God. Meanwhile, the real enemy of our souls roams around our territory winning victory after victory."[16]

David's response qualifies him to be one of God's beautiful people. His inner strength and self-discipline showed in his actions.[17] F. B. Meyer suggests that it was here that David really won his victory over Goliath. To lose his temper in such an unprovoked assault would have broken the alliance of his soul with God and drawn a veil over David's sense of His presence.[18] Those who are gentlest under provocation are strongest in the fight. Meekness is really an attribute of might. As Chambers says: "It is impossible to enter into communion with God when you are in a critical temper."

How do you respond when others show more spiritual passion than you do? When they have more talents than you? more energy than you? more initiative, gifts, opportunities, or ideas? How do you respond when others have less spiritual passion than you do? when no one shares your vision? when you're attacked for being who you are in the Lord? when your passion for God is intimidating, misunderstood, or misinterpreted— seen as fanatical? Passion is usually provocative. It can be unsettling, irritating, and create resistance in those not sharing it or understanding it. At times passion for God can be a very lonely experience.

How David responded says something about his inner private world—his sense of self, well-being, and passion. Having nothing to prove and nothing to lose, he refused to get caught up in the "measuring yourself by others" game or life's "king of the mountain" kind of stuff. Neither ridicule nor those who didn't understand or share his passion could stop David. He first had to contend with his older brother's attitudes, then with King Saul's put-downs, and finally with Goliath's demeaning words.[19] I call the situation "David and the 'three dwarfs.'" I find parallels between David and Joseph—both experienced family criticism prior to saving God's people.[20] Both could have had their passion for God sapped by very draining people, but they had their focus elsewhere.

Is there a message for us in the way Scripture juxtaposes David and Goliath earlier in the story? I think so. "David went back and forth from Saul to tend his father's flock at Bethlehem. The Philistine came forward morning and evening for forty days and took his stand" (1 Sam. 17:15, 16,

NASB). In the hills and pastures of Bethlehem David, as he tended his father's sheep, immersed himself in the immensity and immediacy of God. He had practiced the presence of God so much that he could stay focused on the real issues and deal graciously with his older brother. Thus David remained undaunted by Eliab's criticisms because he took God's word over the opinions of others. That's what passion is all about. Passion chooses who or what it listens to, hears only what it wants to hear. It will not open itself indiscriminately to just any voice or influence. David chose God's voice above all others.

[1] F. B. Meyer, *The Life of David,* p. 33.
[2] Keith Kaynor, *When God Chooses,* p. 42.
[3] F. W. Krummacher, *David, King of Israel,* p. 44.
[4] Robert P. Gordon, *I and II Samuel: A Commentary* (Grand Rapids: Zondervan Publishing House, 1986), p. 156.
[5] Ellen G. White, *Patriarchs and Prophets,* p. 645.
[6] Walter Bruggemann, *David's Truth in Israel's Imagination and Memory,* p. 32.
[7] Gordon, p. 156.
[8] Theodore H. Epp, *A Man After the Heart of God,* p. 14.
[9] Oswald Chambers, *My Utmost for His Highest,* reading for June 17, p. 123.
[10] Gordon MacDonald, *Restoring Your Spiritual Passion,* p. 97.
[11] *Ibid.,* p. 101.
[12] *Ibid.,* pp. 84-91.
[13] C. D. Bryan, *Friendly Fire* (New York: G. P. Putnam's Sons, 1976).
[14] *Ibid.,* p. 51.
[15] MacDonald, p. 94.
[16] Charles R. Swindoll, *David: A Man of Passion and Destiny,* p. 43.
[17] Kaynor, p. 44.
[18] Meyer, p. 37.
[19] Epp, p. 14.
[20] Robert D. Bergen, *1, 2 Samuel,* p. 193.

6

IS THERE NOT A CAUSE?

I Samuel 17:20-30

When Arnold Lehman, director of the Brooklyn Museum of Art, negotiated to bring the art exhibition "Sensation: Young British Artists From the Saatchi Collection" to Brooklyn, he was hoping to bring some life back into the museum's flagging attendance figures. In London on business, Lehman happened to catch the "Sensation" show at the Royal Academy. It was creating a furor, and lines to see it stretched around the block. "You had young kids with green hair, and you had the charming older ladies," he recalls. "People were truly enthralled." Much of the art was indeed sensational, starting with Damien Hirst's carcasses of a cow and pig. Hirst sliced the animals into sections to reveal the innards and suspended the body parts in sequence in tanks of formaldehyde. Visitors could see the full cow or pig and walk between the parts viewing their innards. Marc Quinn fashioned a death mask cast replica of his own head and filled it with eight pints of his own frozen blood—kept cool, of course, in a refrigerated case. Marcus Harvey created a giant grisaille portrait of an English child abuser and murderer, Myra Hindley, out of child-sized handprints. With these kinds of exhibits in mind, Lehman ordered up a buzz-seeking ad campaign that included a mock health warning: "The contents of this exhibition may cause shock, vomiting, confusion, panic, euphoria and anxiety."

89

By the time the ad campaign was in full swing New York City mayor Rudy Giuliani came out slugging. During a press conference he blasted the show. A reporter had brought to his attention that one of the pieces of art to go on exhibition was *The Holy Virgin Mary,* a painting by Chris Ofili, who used, among other materials, elephant dung to create her picture of Mary. According to the media, she had smeared the sacred icon with animal feces. Giuliani, a Roman Catholic, minced no words: "This is sick stuff and offensive." "You don't have a right to government subsidy for desecrating somebody else's religion." The mayor then threatened to cut all city funding to the museum—$7 million a year, about a third of its operating budget—unless it canceled the show.[1]

When David heard Goliath shouting his threats and cursing the God of Israel, he was livid. He found the giant's dramatic presentation—complete with costume, actions, and words—deeply disturbing. "Who is this uncircumcised Philistine, that he should taunt the armies of the living God?" he impulsively asked with telltale dismay and anger (1 Sam. 17:26, NASB). Even the casual reader notices the difference between the tenor of David's instinctive response to Goliath and the fear-driven reaction of every other Israelite in the valley of Elah. Every morning and evening Goliath would stand between the two armies and defy any Israelite, including Saul, to come out and fight. In the process, the Philistine warrior rejected the reality and potency of Israel's God. Apparently the giant was all that the Israelites were looking at or could think about afterward. Their vision did not go beyond this giant of a man who frightened them, shamed them, and laughed at their God. Not so with David.

From the moment he heard Goliath's challenge, he realized that the Philistine warrior was not only challenging Israel's army, but the living God as well.[2] In David's mind, to attack Israel was to wage war against God.[3] To bad-mouth Israel was to insult the Lord. Thus to belittle Israel was to belittle its God. David says as much when he goes out to meet the blasphemous bigmouth: "You come against me with sword and spear and javelin, but I come against you in the name of the Lord Almighty, the God of the armies of Israel, whom you have defied" (verse 45, NIV).

The Hebrew word for *taunted* occurs five times in the story (verses 10, 25, 26, 36, 45). It refers to an offensive act that berates, scorns, heaps shame on someone, mocks them, or belittles them. In David's mind

Goliath was essentially mocking Israel's God—no wonder he couldn't help blurting out, "Who is this uncircumcised Philistine, that he should taunt the armies of the living God?" His question obviously implies, "How dare he defy?" or "Who does this Philistine think he is, anyway?" (Defiance and casting shame have to do with what or who we think we are and what we think about God.) On another level, though, David was insinuating something entirely different, "How can you let this mocking go unanswered? Huh? No one talks this way about God. So why is everybody running?" That's David's point—Israel needed to do something about Goliath's bad-mouthing God besides just cowering and running. They couldn't let the giant's taunts go unanswered. "This is God we're talking about here!" His question puts the challenge in its proper theological perspective—the reputation of "the living God."[4]

Is There Not a Cause?

David, then, is jealous for God's name and reputation. He is fired with zeal to preserve the honor of the living God and to maintain the relationship of God's people with their Lord.[5] Because his eyes were on God, his heart reacted instinctively to the blasphemous utterances of the great Philistine.[6] This is why David would not be sidetracked when Eliab put him down with a big-brother tongue-lashing. "Why have you come down here? And with whom did you leave those few sheep in the desert? I know how conceited you are and how wicked your heart is; you came down only to watch the battle" (verse 28, NIV). Eliab said everything he could to discourage David and put him down. But the younger brother's only response to Eliab's insinuations is to say, "Hey, what have I done now? All I did was ask a question" (see verse 29). Then he simply turns away and walks over to another group of soldiers and asks them the same question he'd been raising earlier: "What will a man get for killing this Philistine and putting an end to his abuse of Israel? Who is this pagan Philistine, anyway, that he is allowed to defy the armies of the living God?" (see verses 26, 30). The concluding clause of David's response to Eliab is brief but problematic.[7] Major contemporary versions translate the literal Hebrew—"[Is] it not [a] word/matter?"—in various ways. The New King James Version has David asking a question: "Is there not a cause?" The New Revised Standard Version has him saying, "It was only a question." And the New International Version reads, "Can't I even speak?" I prefer the New King James Version's question—"Is there not a cause?"—because it captures the essence of the overarching issue.

Why did David ask his questions? Why did he want to speak up? Because there existed a compelling cause that needed championing. Here's how I envision the meaning of David's response to Eliab: "What have I done? All I did was ask a question. Isn't there something more important to be concerned about here than me? Something that really matters—like that giant out there? A cause to champion?" David knew where the real issue lay—the honor and glory of God and a blaspheming giant that needed silencing.

"Is there not a cause?" That's the question passion inevitably asks! "Is there not a cause today to stand up for? Some great purpose that draws me like a magnet and compels me to champion something, to stand behind, support, and trumpet it? A cause that involves the meaning of my life, the purpose of my existence—where all else pales by comparison?" Passion has purpose, a reason for being, an agenda. Some lofty crusade it is willing to spend and be spent for. Without a cause or reason for being, passion is either impossible or empty—mere emotionalism, zeal without knowledge or real purpose.

Passion for God also inevitably demands, "Is there not something today for us to stand up for and be firm in the faith of the Lord Jesus Christ?" It is not a matter of going out and fighting with others or of attacking personalities, but of getting into the midst of the spiritual battle with the living God of heaven so that those who ridicule and defy Him will no longer go unchallenged—either in our minds or by our words, actions, lifestyle, or witness. We can make a difference. Not only was God defamed and belittled in David's day, but He faces similar charges today.[8]

Our politically correct postmodern world allows for and even nurtures all kinds of crude defiance and demeaning of Christian faith and values. Consider two recent parodies of Leonardo da Vinci's mural of the Lord's Supper. One called *Yo Mama's Last Supper* features a nude woman standing at the table as Christ (everyone else is sitting), arms outstretched with linen draped over her forearms. The other titled *The Last Pancake Breakfast* has Mrs. Butterworth standing in for Jesus and cereal cartoon figures representing disciples.[9]

Whether it is music, the arts, movies, humor, or politics, we find God, purity, biblical truth, integrity, sanctity of marriage, Christianity, or our Adventist hope and heritage mocked and defied. How do we respond? When we hear people within our own ranks saying certain standards or biblical teachings belong to an older, less mature, less educated generation, is there not a cause? A sobering vision in Ezekiel depicts the Lord telling a man clothed in linen and with an inkhorn at his side to "go through the midst of the city, even through the midst of Jerusalem, and put a mark on the foreheads of the men who sigh and groan over all the abominations which are being committed in its midst" (Eze. 9:4, NASB). In other words, it was a time when even Israel's religious leaders violated God's laws and defiled holy things through their actions and worship of false gods. They confused the line between the sacred and profane, making evil look holy and holy things commonplace (Eze. 22:26). But not everybody compromised. God took special note of those who felt there was a cause to be saddened over and to stand in the gap for.

As Potiphar's wife tried to seduce Joseph, he regarded sexual purity, the sanctity of marriage, and the honor of God to be a cause worthy to stand up for (Gen. 39:7-9). When Nebuchadnezzar placed his choicest foods at Daniel's table for him to eat or Darius's decree forbade worship to anyone but him, Daniel thought what he ate and the rhythm of his devotional life was a cause to stand up for (Dan. 1:8-16; 6:1-28). At Baal Peor Phinehas saw one of the young princes of Israel brazenly taking a Midianite prostitute into his tent—right in front of everyone. Phinehas considered the separation of God's people from the pagan world in terms of music, entertainment, and lifestyle something to stand up for. In response, he took a javelin and impaled the couple together on the tent floor (Num. 25:6-11). Scripture, by the way, tells us that Phinehas was jealous with God's jealousy (verse 11). God's passion for His people fueled his passion.

The powerful religious leaders of Martin Luther's day harangued and threatened him for the positions he had taken on Scripture and justification by faith, but he thought them worth standing up for. Didn't Jesus view it as a cause to stand for when He told the church at Thyatira "I have this against you: you tolerate that woman Jezebel, who calls herself a prophet and is teaching and beguiling my servants to practice fornication and to eat food sacrificed to idols" (Rev. 2:20, NRSV). Whenever I read that passage I ask myself, "Larry, what Jezebel are you tolerating in your life, your ministry, your congregation, your family? Is there some passion-draining dysfunction, situation, habit, belief, or attitude that you are not actively challenging or opposing?" Is there not a cause?

We live in an age when many hesitate to take a stand or position. They are afraid of being labeled either legalistic or fanatical. But passion for a cause need be neither legalistic nor fanatical. It can simply be the right thing to do, because God's reputation and work are on trial. We should be sensitive to people but clear on the issues. Sometimes all we can do is to react inwardly because we cannot change the people or circumstances around us.

Like David, our greatest concerns should be to uphold God's reputation. We call ourselves Seventh-day Adventist Christians. But how concerned are we that as His representatives on earth we constantly and consistently bring honor to His name? Do we have a heart like David? passion for God like David? How do we respond when someone talks negatively about God, His revealed will, His church, or the lifestyle He calls us to live and preach in these last days? When someone disparages His work or ministries, does it stir indignation and a passion to uphold what is true, and lovely, and right, and clean, and pure, and good? How do you react when the unbelieving and rebellious world around us defies God? How do you feel when people around you lack faith? Isn't God defied by a lack of faith on the part of many who profess to believe in Him?[10]

Do you have a cause? In other words, what are you living for? What is the purpose of your life, your reason for being? your passion? What kind of deep motivational drive shapes your vision? Is it God? We all have some cause that we follow, but is it always the right one? Is it God and His character, His work, will, and people? I'm talking not about sacred cows, but about a sacred cause. The Pharisees of Jesus' day were into sacred cows—their traditions and comfort zones. Sometimes our passion or the cause we take a stand for involves more what we're used to or how we've been raised rather than the will of God or His honor or obedience to Scripture. Is the passion of your life some cause (sacred cow) or is your passion God's honor? That calls for some heart-searching, don't you think? Paul understood that passion has purpose when he wrote: "So whether you eat or drink or whatever you do, do it all for the glory of God" (1 Cor. 10:31, NIV).

Ellen White profoundly articulates such passion: "The greatest want of this age is the want of men—men who will not be bought or sold; men who are true and honest in their inmost souls; men who will not fear to call sin by its right name, and to condemn it, in themselves or in others; men whose conscience is as true to duty as the needle to the pole; men who will stand for the right, though the heavens fall."[11] This is passion with purpose. Passion for God.

There Are No Shortcuts

When Goliath challenged the armies of Israel he became a symbol of the Philistines' threat to Israel's continued existence as the Lord's people. As the giant issued his challenge, he took his place in the long line of those who in their arrogance have thought that they could defy the Living God.[12] Thus when David went out to battle Goliath, he didn't go as a daring young man in search of personal glory but because he felt that the honor of the Lord was at stake. He was concerned only that all the earth would know that there was a God in Israel (1 Sam. 17:46).[13] *Is that my passion?* I wonder to myself. *That the world would know that there is a God in my life, my home, my church, my world? How would that passion-driven vision change my life?*

But how do we get this kind of passion? How do we see through the moral and spiritual fog and grasp the right cause? How do we come to the place in our lives where God's name, honor, reputation, and glory become a burning passion in the soul? And how do we find strength to stand up for God when everyone else is running from Goliath? It comes down to where our hearts are focused—to what we allow ourselves to see and hear. Remember, now, at this point in the story of David it is the forty-first day that the Israelites have encountered Goliath. But this is the first time David has heard the big-mouthed brute. While David's heart burns with a holy indignation, the passion for God in Eliab and Saul and others has diminished—if not vanished altogether. Could it be because they had listened to Goliath's taunts for 40 days? Does the longer that we go on hearing defiance, lack of faith, criticism, taunting, negativism, gossip, demeaning of truth or biblical standards—whatever—the weaker we get and the stronger the enemy becomes in our own eyes? I think so. When we allow others to go on and on defying God without some kind of personal stand for His glory, we become too paralyzed to do anything. As with Eliab, Saul, and most every other Israelite in the valley of Elah that day, we lose a sense of the holy and of who God is. We need a restored passion for God's name, reputation, and cause. But how do we get it?

While the army of Israel spent 40 days listening to Goliath, David had been immersing himself in the immenseness and immediacy of God. There at Bethlehem, while tending his father's sheep, David shaped his imagination and heart around a vision of God's creative power and presence. In those quiet moments of meditating, singing, praying, and worship, his sense of God became more vivid. The Lord was as real to David as Jesse or his brothers or Saul or Goliath. This is the unfailing secret of passion with ultimate purpose—God! Revelation tells of four living creatures and 24 elders caught up with the incredible image of God's creative power and redeeming grace. Day and night they praise the living God. In their opinion, He is worthy to receive glory, honor, power, riches, wisdom, might, dominion, blessing, and worship (Rev. 4:8-11; 5:12-14). How impassioned would I be for God if I beheld Him as clearly and consistently as they? The life of passion for God and His honor has no shortcuts. We must have periods of lonely meditation and fellowship with God, filling our minds with His Word.[14] Ellen White advises that "in an age like ours, in which iniquity abounds, and God's character and His law are alike regarded with contempt, special care must be taken to teach the youth to study, to reverence and obey the divine will as revealed to man. The fear of the Lord is fading from the minds of our youth because of their neglect of Bible study."[15]

Is there a cause? How have you been standing up for God? Is He worth the price? Often standing for the Lord, having a passion for His honor and glory, doing battle with the giants, is a lonely experience. It comes only when, like David, we have attached our hearts to Him.

The conditions in and around us shape our passion for God. But the people who populate our personal worlds also affect our passion. MacDonald lists five kinds of people that influence our passion for God: (1) the very *resourceful* people who *ignite* our passion, sometimes called mentors; (2) the very *important* people who *share* our passion because they are close friends or work closely with us in God's work; (3) the very *trainable* people who can *catch* our passion and, as they do, can stir our own passion to serve and grow (now we become the ones who ignite passion); (4) the very *nice* people who merely *enjoy* our passion and who neither add to it nor diminish it; and (5) the very *draining* people who *sap* our passion because their relationship to us is usually on the minus side of the flow of energy.[16]

Norman W. Dunn was one of those highly resourceful people who ignited my passion for God when, as a young ministerial intern, I was assigned to the Seventh-day Adventist church in Luray, Virginia. Norman's influence in my life often guides/leads my heart even today. I can still hear his raspy voice and picture his elfish, square build topped by a bulldog face and shiny bald head. He'd grab me by the elbow and cock his head to peer deeply into my eyes. With a stubby finger wagging at my cheek, he'd share what was passionately consuming him at the moment.

Everything Norman did was with passion. He talked and laughed and even drank "dram"—his own soda-water and apple-juice mix—with passion. But even more intensely, he prayed, spoke of God, and worked for Him with passion. Norman's 47 years of uninterrupted ministry in the United States, South America, Inter-America, and finally as part of the world leadership of the General Conference of Seventh-day Adventists, was in stark contrast to this young intern from backwoods Pennsylvania. I had neither denominational heritage nor breadth of experience. In fact, I hardly had seen anywhere beyond small-town U.S.A.

When I met Norman, he was happily retired but still energetically at work for God. He visited his neighbors, gave personal Bible studies, and knew his community. Loving God's cause, he attended every church function that needed his support. Norman longed to see God's work finished. Anxiously watching the activities of his world church, he would often offer his personal commentary on the onward progress of God's work. Passionate appeals for those who carried the responsibilities of leading the church he loved filled his prayers.

Thus, I realize now, his interest in me. He reached out to me with a clear sense of influencing my young life and ministry. Norman gave me an awareness of the breadth of God's church and our mission in the world. In the process he helped form my attitudes toward God's people and the gospel ministry.

To this day I have never forgotten two of the most distinct mentoring moments he provided me. I was holding my first evangelistic crusade in a tiny rural church. Our average attendance was 12. The experience was a ministerial exercise designed to cut my evangelistic teeth. For 27 nights I spoke to a gray-haired audience who already believed everything I was preaching and were convinced they knew most of it better than I did.

Norman drove the winding country roads every night to show his support and offer his perspective. Before each meeting he would pull me aside, thrust his stubby finger into my face, and rasp his encouragement. "Keep throwing out the net. Keep throwing out the net. One of these days you will pull it back in, and there'll be a fish in it!"

True to his convictions, God blessed. Near the end of those mind-numbing weeks, a new face showed conspicuously among the familiar handful. Soon afterward, Mary was baptized. It was a decision that would ripple across many years, affecting an entire family. But the net Norman helped to throw out will prove, in eternity, to hold much, much more than a single fish.

At every evangelistic meeting I've ever been involved in, the image of Norman whispering his passionate encouragement has reminded me of the simple role I have in the grand plan to save souls—to keep "throwing out the net." I've said it to myself and to anxious young interns, and I've reminded my tired colleagues of it.

The second mentoring moment occurred when Norman signed over his 27-volume set of *The Pulpit Commentary*. I had seen the set in his library and longed for one of my own, but I didn't have that kind of money. One day I asked if I could use a volume for a sermon I was preparing. Always eager to help, Norman was buoyant as he lent it to me. "If you sign in blood," he whispered threateningly. Soon I was regularly borrowing from his small library. One day I made a bold proposal. "Norman, I'm in active ministry and could make good use of these. Don't you think I need them more than you do?" My question caught him off guard. But his surprise soon turned into a wry smile. Wagging that finger, he rasped, "If you talk just right, I'll give them to you."

I didn't know what I needed to say in order to qualify, but I saw in those books a symbol of Norman's ministry, his commitment, his passion. They represented the torch of his ministry as much as a sermon resource.

That's why I was moved beyond words the day I went to borrow a volume, and he had them all boxed up by his front door. It was an event to commemorate with a shot of "dram." As we sipped his brew, he talked about the cause of God. Eagerly Norman reached into the top box and handed me volume one. I wept as I read his message, written in bold, definitive strokes—words that carried the passion of his heart.

"To my cherished young friend Larry Lichtenwalter I give this treasured *Pulpit Commentary* because—

"1. I vividly recall my own ardent longing for such a mine of biblical information at the beginning of my ministry, yet, in spite of my desperate need, 'no man gave unto me.'

"2. I have observed in Larry two basic traits which must never be lacking in a minister, namely, (a) an eagerness for a thorough knowledge of the Word, and (b) a wholehearted devotion to the Author of the Word.

"3. By 'talking just right' during the past few months, Larry has convinced me that more people will be benefited if I now place this rich source of information at his disposal, rather than keep it for personal use, with the idea of giving these books to him when my opportunity for public preaching has ended.

"Therefore, much as I love this commentary, I gladly give these books to Larry, assured in my heart that he will persevere in his search for truth to transmit to others.

"Sincerely,

"Norman W. Dunn

"Dec. 1975."

"Is there a cause?" Certainly! And God filled men such as Norman with an understanding of what that cause must ever be—God, His character, His glory, His work. Passion has purpose. O that the cause of God would ever inflame the passion of my heart for Him! And you? What purpose drives your soul? What cause calls you forth?

---

[1] Cathleen Mcguigan, "A Shock Grows in Brooklyn," *Newsweek*, Oct. 11, 1999, pp. 68-70; Steven Henry Madoff, "Shock for Shock's Sake?" *Time*, Oct. 11, 1999, pp. 80-82.
[2] Theodore H. Epp, *A Man After the Heart of God*, p. 12.
[3] Gene A. Getz, *David: Seeking God Faithfully*, p. 55.
[4] Ralph W. Klein, *1 Samuel, Word Biblical Commentary*, vol. 10, p. 178.
[5] Ellen G. White, *Patriarchs and Prophets*, p. 645.
[6] *Ibid.*

[7] Robert D. Bergen, *1, 2 Samuel*, p. 193.

[8] Epp, p. 15.

[9] "Right Now, It's 'Supper' Time," *Newsweek*, Mar. 5, 2001, p. 9.

[10] *Ibid.*, p. 17.

[11] Ellen G. White, in *Signs of the Times*, May 4, 1882.

[12] Holmes Rolston, *Personalities Around David* (Richmond, Va.: John Knox Press, 1968), p. 26.

[13] Rolston, p. 27.

[14] F. B. Meyer, *The Life of David*, p. 35.

[15] Ellen G. White, *Counsels to Parents, Teachers, and Students* (Mountain View, Calif.: Pacific Press Pub. Assn., 1913), p. 89.

[16] Gordon MacDonald, *Restoring Your Spiritual Passion*, pp. 71-91.

7

HOW TO CARRY A GIANT'S HEAD

I Samuel 17:40-51, 54

The story of David and Goliath is one of the greatest of all children's stories. It's the first full-blown story about David, and by far the most memorable. If you know anything about David, it is probably his encounter with the giant.

David's weapon of choice against Goliath—the sling—provided him with a tremendous advantage over any of the weapons the Philistine warrior had at his disposal. Every one of Goliath's weapons was of value only in close combat. Even then, they could be cumbersome. Take his spear, for example. Because its tip alone weighed nearly 15 pounds, he could not have employed it effectively against an opponent standing more than a few feet away. On the other hand, David could use his sling with deadly force from comparatively great distances. With his youthful vigor and unencumbered by heavy armor and weaponry, he could dash to locations from which he could hurl the tennis-ball-sized stones directly at Goliath. Slingstones were not little marbles. Many of the stones in the creekbed in the valley of Elah are like little cannonballs. I've knelt there and picked up a few of those fist-sized specimens, trying to imagine being wacked in the head by a rock that size. Slingers could achieve great accuracy. The left-handed Benjamites could sling a stone at a hair and not miss (Judges 20:16). The average speed of a slingstone would be somewhere around 100 miles per hour. It's no wonder that modern-day

Israelis are fearful of Palestinian slingers. The technique sounds so primitive and ineffective until you understand its deadly accuracy.

Taking a single stone from his shepherd's bag, David felled the Philistine with ease and deadly accuracy. The slingstone struck with such great force that it crushed the frontal bone of Goliath's cranium and "sank into his forehead" (1 Sam. 17:49, NIV).[1] The surprised giant reeled with pain as he fell to his knees, then blacked out facedown in the field.

The story, though, doesn't end with the sling and the slingstone, but with the head in David's hand. Scripture tells us that he immediately ran and stood over Goliath. Drawing the giant's own sword from its scabbard, he killed him with it. Then David chopped off the giant's head (verse 51). I can imagine Goliath lying facedown in the field and David kicking his arms backward toward the warrior's torso in order to clearly expose his neck for a clear chop. And he didn't just wack Goliath's head off and leave it at that. David reached down and grabbed the severed head by the hair and raised it up for all to see. I think he showed it to his fellow Israelites first—the ones who had been so fearful. Then swinging around and holding it high, he waved it in front of the Philistines. We can only imagine the grotesque spectacle—warm crimson blood still dripping from the severed head, perhaps trickling down on David's legs, bulging eyes staring from their sockets, a stone embedded in a collapsed and bleeding forehead.

Stripping a dead man of his weapon and decapitating his corpse was part of the battlefield customs of David's day (cf. 1 Sam. 31:9). Beheading was a way of dishonoring a corpse[2] as well as undeniable proof that the guy was dead. If you hold up your enemy's head by the hair, he's gone! It's the epitome of mockery and gloating. My imagination stirred with the reality of such a sight when I saw a World War II photo of a native Philippine soldier holding a giant's head. It's a black-and-white picture taken outside the city of Manila in a little village called San Antorius near Barryos, part of a collection of pictures from my father's tour of military duty during that tragic era. The head was that of a Japanese Imperial Marine soldier. Japanese Imperial Marines were usually six feet six inches or taller, a stature then highly unusual for Japanese. The Philippine soldier, a short, slightly built man, was holding the decapitated head by both ears. The proportions of his little body and the massive head made for an unusual picture. Such decapitations and other body mutilations were in response to the earlier rape of Manila by the Japanese. This Philippine soldier regarded himself as an agent of retribution. For him, holding the enemy's head like a trophy was a powerful moment of triumph.

David carried the grotesque souvenir with him when he went to see King Saul. Picture David as he stands there before the fainthearted king "with the Philistine's head in his hand," holding it like some kind of trophy (1 Sam. 17:57, NASB). As the flabbergasted Saul asks, "Whose son are you, young man?" David stands there with the giant's head in his hand. "I am the son of your servant Jesse the Bethlehemite," he says (verse 58, NKJV). What a sight that must have been. It was both embarrassing and astonishing to every fainthearted person there—including Saul's commander of the army, Abner. Interestingly, David had often been in Saul's home. He had played the harp to soothe the king. The king even wanted to keep him there full-time. Now, though, Saul is so taken aback by the turn of events and David's bravery that he's not really sure who David is. *This can't be my musician.* "Whose's son are you, young man?" Everyone is shaken by the sudden turn of events—and the giant's head.

David carried Goliath's head the nearly 17 miles or so to Jerusalem (verse 54). Can you imagine carrying a severed head while trekking so many miles? Why did David do it, and why to Jerusalem? At the time, the city was not under Israelite control. It was still in the hands of Israel's long-time enemy, the Jebusites (2 Sam. 5:6-9; 1 Sam. 17:57). Some suggest David brought the gruesome remains of Israel's most feared enemy there in order to intimidate the city's inhabitants. Mounting Goliath's head in a conspicuous location, or throwing it over the wall into the city, as some suggest, would have certainly demonstrated to this longtime enemy that there was indeed a God in Israel.[3] David was brazenly putting them on notice that someday he'd have their heads too. He was staking out his territory. It is no coincidence that David's first offensive military campaign after becoming Israel's king was to take Jerusalem and claim it as his new capital.

The idea of David carrying Goliath's head is both incomprehensible and appalling to our modern way of thinking. But the imagery is awesome. God wants each one of us to carry the head of the spiritual giant that browbeats, bullies, intimidates, and terrorizes our lives and keeps us from being and doing what He has envisioned for us. Even the great controversy between Christ and Satan revolves around the promise that only the

Messiah's heel would be bruised, but the serpent's head would be crushed (Gen. 3:15). Only when one has removed the head from the body does it fully eradicate the threat or potential of someone's return. That's why people throughout history have hung heads to rot while they buried bodies.

The Lord not only wants us to remove the heads of the spiritual giants that intimidate us, but desires that we carry them around as symbols of our complete victory over them. For example, God wants us to put on display the heads of such giants as fear and worry. Other giants come in the shapes of temptation, social pressure, or the unknown. Sometimes they manifest themselves in the form of a person or of a weakness that we feel. They can be fear that hammers on your heart every morning and every night, day in and day out, yelling across the ravine in your own personal valley of Elah.

Dominating Imagination

How do you carry a giant's head? It boils down to one word—imagination, the reality that fills our inner private world. Imagination is the world of pictures within us.[4] The human mind is a picture gallery. Imagination consists of the images that haunt our perception of reality. Are they about God? Or Goliath? As we examine the details of this story we will find ourselves faced with the challenge of acquiring a God-dominated imagination and rejecting a Goliath-filled one.[5]

When David showed up at Ephes-dammim and joined Saul's encampment in the valley of Elah, Goliath commanded the situation. The warrior's most remarkable feature was his height: "six cubits and a span" (1 Sam. 17:4). Somewhere near nine feet nine inches tall, he was an enormous man. The NBA would love him! And if you add to his height the length of his arms when he would raise them over his head, you can imagine what an imposing being he must have been. Undoubtedly, his physical stature was awesome and psychologically overpowering to the typically small Israelites.

Adding to Goliath's overwhelming appearance as a fighter was his combat gear and weaponry.[6] The giant was sheathed in metal. He covered his head with "a bronze helmet" (verse 5, NIV)[7] and wore a heavy canvaslike garment interlaced with overlapping ringlets of bronze ("a coat of scale armor of bronze weighing five thousand shekels" [verse 5, NIV]). We would call it a coat of mail. This flexible armor went from shoulder to knee, covering and protecting against the enemy's weapons. Bronze leggings protected his shins and knees. Slung over his back was a curved bronze sword or throwing spear called a javelin (verse 6). In his hand he carried a longer spear whose "shaft was like a weaver's rod" (verse 7, NIV). At the head of Goliath's spear was a massive iron point that weighed 600 shekels, nearly 15 pounds. A weapon of this massive weight, while quite awkward to use, would be intimidating in appearance—probably its main purpose. However, it could crack a skull easily, and the momentum from thrusting and swinging would be enough to knock any ordinary-sized fellow over. As double protection against arrows, Goliath had a "shield carrier" walking in front of him, carrying a shield the size of a full-grown man.

Pause for a moment and allow your mind to picture the imposing sight. Imagine how frightening it would be to take on a giant of this size and protected by this amount of armor.

Now a coat of mail of the weight and composition Goliath wore would have drastically reduced his ability to respond quickly and with agility in close combat. It suggests that Goliath may not have really expected a skirmish involving hand-to-hand combat with anyone close to an equal.[8] The giant's appearance, complete with costume, actions, and words, was a dramatic show, an act of psychological warfare. Intent on capturing and dominating Israel's imagination, he wanted to become the polestar around which everyone took their bearings.[9] And it worked! "Saul and all Israel . . . were dismayed, and greatly afraid" (verse 11). The front lines literally fled in terror when Goliath bellowed out his taunts and began striding up the ravine toward them (verse 24).

Goliath didn't issue his challenge one time and then leave. It was a 40-day in-your-face kind of thing (verse 16). Every morning and every evening for more than a month Goliath marched out into the open, flaunting his size and his strength and his weaponry, daring someone to take him on. That's the way with giants. They don't come just once, but morning and evening, day after day, relentlessly trying to intimidate us. In the process they dominate our imagination, ultimately taking over our sense of reality. Goliath's evening and morning tirade coincided with Israel's call to worship, likely interrupting their spiritual focus during a time their hearts should have been turning to God. Giants love to interrupt worship. They confuse or occupy our minds with fearful imaginings until we can no longer focus on God.

Often they distract us from worship altogether—both personal and corporate. Eugene Peterson asserts that "the moment we permit evil to control our imagination, dictate the way we think, and shape our responses, we at the same time become incapable of seeing the good and the true and the beautiful."[10] And we become too paralyzed to withstand.

David entered the valley of Elah with a God-dominated imagination, not a Goliath-ruled one. God was the reality with which David lived. Giants didn't figure largely in David's understanding of the real world.[11] As Peterson observes, when David tended the family flocks around Bethlehem, he "was immersed in the largeness and immediacy of God. He had experienced God's strength in protecting the sheep in his fights with lions and bears. He had practiced the presence of God so thoroughly that God's word, which he couldn't literally hear, was far more real to him than the lion's roar, which he could hear. He had worshiped the majesty of God so continuously that God's love, which he couldn't see, was far more real to him than the bear's ferocity, which he could see. His praying and singing, his meditation and adoration had shaped an imagination in him that set each sheep and lamb, bear and lion into something large and vast and robust: God."[12] The only giant in David's life was God. To the shepherd-musician, Goliath was a mere dwarf—in league with the wild beasts he had already encountered (verse 36). Everyone around David thought, *The Philistine is too big to kill.* But David mused, *Goliath is too big to miss!*

Imagination makes the difference in our passion for God. Whatever dominates it either affects or determines our passion for God. Our imagination involves the images that haunt our perception of reality. The reality that occupies our inner private world will become our passion. If God fills our imagination, then He will be our passion. But passion haunts imagination as well. It centers our imagination. When God is our passion, He will soon shape our imagination. Once passion for something awakens to the point that it dominates our perception of reality, it will imprint our imagination with that very image. This is much deeper and broader than the link between passion and imagination that we've examined earlier. There we saw passion as filling the heart with art. Once you have passion your imagination kicks in. Nothing is boring, colorless, or remains status quo. Instead, there emerges inspiration, vision, invention, and creativity. Remember how David's heart produced incredible art—poetry and music?

Here, though, we're not talking about passion being imaginative, but rather how passion haunts and thus focuses that imagination. Imagination is more than mere creativity. Something fundamentally deeper, it's what orients our being and our vision of reality. It involves how we see the world—both in terms of the natural and the supernatural, the material and personal, humanity and God. Creativity flows from this vision of reality, but such creativity cannot be enduring if either our sense of reality is not focused by our passion or our passion is not directed by our sense of reality. When passion *claims it all* and *yields it all* for some compelling cause, experience, object, being, or relationship, imagination frames everything one does. It becomes the world in which we live, and everything revolves around it.

David's passion for God so haunted his imagination that God Himself came to fill it with compelling presence. Israel's future king was so immersed in God's immenseness and immediacy that the Lord became more real to him than anything else. That's passion.

Carrying a Giant's Head

How do you carry a giant's head? How does the kind of passion that haunts our imagination become a reality in our lives?

If you want to carry a giant's head, you need to practice the presence of God. Imagine with me David kneeling at the brook to collect stones for his sling. The text doesn't say that he bent down to get them, only that he "chose five smooth stones" (verse 40, NIV). But he must have knelt to select the stones, feeling and testing each one for balance and size. And he did it in full view of everyone, unprotected and vulnerable. I am sure David wasn't thinking only about slingstones but also about God and the enemy. He was concerned about his passion for God's honor and the integrity of the Lord's people—that everyone would know there is a God in Israel. David at that moment did something that's absolutely essential for each of us also to do. Like him, we have to find answers to vital questions: Are we going to live this life from our knees, imaginatively and personally—with God? Are we going to be shaped by our fears of Goliath or by God?[13]

We've already learned about David the commuter. All of us need to become aware of God's presence and activity both in the world and in our lives. David had an education that Goliath knew nothing of and that Saul had sadly neglected. The shepherd-musician had trained in a divine school that specialized in preparing the heart through the Word and through personal communion with the Lord. Thus David's public victories were the product of his private and secret fellowship with God.[14] The song says it well: "Only a boy named David, only a little sling, only a boy named David, but he could pray and sing." David met God in private, and thereby conquered the foe in private. As a result he defeated the foe in public.[15] When you focus on God and what He can do, you think differently. Passion that practices the presence of God stirs imagination.

If you want to carry a giant's head, you need to experience the power of God in smaller things. When David said to Saul, "Let no man's heart fail on account of him; your servant will go and fight with this Philistine" (verse 32, NASB), the king tried to dissuade him, saying, "You are not able to go against this Philistine to fight with him; for you are but a youth while he has been a warrior from his youth" (verse 33, NASB). What a put-down. You are not able! You're just a kid! David's answer is enlightening: "Your servant was tending his father's sheep. When a lion or a bear came and took a lamb from the flock, I went out after him and attacked him, and rescued it from his mouth; and when he rose up against me, I seized him by his beard and struck him and killed him. Your servant has killed both the lion and the bear; and this uncircumcised Philistine will be like one of them, since he has taunted the armies of the living God" (verses 34-36, NASB). Experience had strengthened David for this battle.[16] His imagination stirred with the image of a close and powerful God. When he compared Goliath to one of the beasts he had already killed, he was essentially saying that giants are not all that big when we've already seen God working in the smaller things of our life.

Thus if you want to carry a giant's head, you need to experience God at work in your life beforehand. We have nothing to fear for the future unless we forget how God has led and empowered us in the past. Experiencing God at work in our life gives reality to imagination.

If you want to carry a giant's head, you need to take the initiative. I'm intrigued with the image of David running, of taking the lead. When a lion or bear seized a lamb from the flock, David went after it and attacked it. Should the animal turn on him, David grabbed it. He didn't wait or follow at a distance, but took the initiative and responded energetically. In the valley of Elah Goliath crossed the ravine at the base of the valley and approached Israel's lines. Instinctively David raced to meet Goliath (verse 48). Clearly David was the more dynamic combatant.[17] According to the Hebrew text, Goliath merely walked, but David ran. When the giant fell facedown in the open field, David once again dashed to stand over him and behead him (verse 51). His pattern involved taking the initiative. He understood that "if you tolerate Goliath, he'll take over your territory. He'll move into your camp. He'll take your thoughts that normally ought to be on God, and he'll put them on himself. That's why you can't afford to tolerate Giants; you kill them."[18] So if you want to carry a giant's head, you must seize the initiative. You can't wait 40 days—or even one day. As soon as you recognize a giant you need to respond. "Faith is not something that is worn outwardly. It is seen only in its boldness in action."[19] Passion not only leads us to take the initiative, it unleashes our imagination. Imagination always dies on the heels of inactivity.

If you want to carry a giant's head, you must be careful to keep the moral and spiritual issues clear in your thinking. David's reply to Goliath's personal tirade says volumes: "You come to me with sword, spear, and javelin, but I come to you in the name of the Lord Almighty—the God of the armies of Israel, whom you have defied. Today the Lord will conquer you, and I will kill you and cut off your head. And then I will give the dead bodies of your men to the birds and wild animals, and the whole world will know that there is a God in Israel! And everyone will know that the Lord does not need weapons to rescue his people. It is his battle, not ours. The Lord will give you to us!" (verses 45-47, NLT). This wasn't a personal thing between him and the giant. Goliath's attitude and behavior defied God.[20] As a result David went out to battle with him, not as a daring young man in search of personal glory, but because he felt that the honor of the Lord was at stake. David was concerned only that all the earth would know that there was a God in Israel (verse 46).[21] Ellen White notes that he "was fired with zeal to preserve the honor of the living God and the credit of His people."[22] There was a cause, and David knew it.

One commentator suggests that David's choice of a stone to kill Goliath expressed his awareness that Goliath had committed a capital crime by insulting, thus blaspheming, God. According to the Torah, any individual guilty of blasphemy—even a non-Israelite—must be stoned (Lev. 24:16).[23] David understood what Scripture had to say on this particular matter, and because he did, he was empowered to act concretely. Whenever we go deeper in God's Word, being careful to detail the explicit things God has to say on particular matters, we will be able to act concretely against a giant's attempt to take over our territory or move into our camp. We'll see things clearly, and because we do, we will not tolerate such Goliaths. Keeping the biblical issues straight in our thinking authenticates imagination. Passion for God will always lead beyond generalities to the deep things of God's Word.

Finally, if you want to carry a giant's head, you must be sure to cut it off! It's a given that if you don't cut the head off, you can't carry it. Many a time we walk away from a supposedly slain giant, only to see it rise up again. That usually happens because we haven't completed our task. To slay giants, we must not hold back. When it comes to moral and spiritual issues, there must be complete victory or there is no victory at all. Theodore Epp reminds us that we must make sure the victory is complete by taking Goliath's sword and cutting off his head.[24] Ellen White warns us of the danger of allowing unchristian traits to dwell in the heart. "One cherished sin will, little by little, debase the character, bringing all its nobler powers into subjection to the evil desire. The removal of one safeguard from the conscience, the indulgence of one evil habit, one neglect of the high claims of duty, breaks down the defenses of the soul and opens the way for Satan to come in and lead us astray."[25] There comes a time when we must break off some relationship, get rid of some material or object or substance, radically change our routine or lifestyle, in order to walk off the field with a giant's head. Removing the giant's head consummates imagination. God doesn't want us to just knock the giant down or subdue him—Goliaths must die, or we will.

So the Whole World Will Know

In the autumn of 1957 *Sputnik* raced across the Appalachian sky above where the small town of Coalwood, West Virginia, was slowly dying. Faced with an uncertain future, a teenager named Homer Hickam nurtured a dream that had been suddenly and unexpectedly awakened: to send rockets into outer space. Sometimes one dream is enough to light up the whole sky. For Hickam, *Sputnik's* one-minute streak across the October sky was enough to light the passion of a dream within. Until then, he had seemed destined to work in the coal mines as his father did. Coal mining was all he could realistically expect. The extraordinary launch of the Soviet rocket that flashed across the sky changed all that. It fired his imagination to see beyond his foreordained life in a coal-mining town that would literally swallow its men alive. Today Homer Hickam is a retired NASA engineer who consults on aerospace projects that interest him.

Hickam tells how *Sputnik* appeared like a bright little ball, moving majestically across the star field between Appalachian mountain ridgelines. "I stared at it," he writes, "with no less rapt attention than if it had been God Himself in a golden chariot riding overhead. It soared with what seemed to me inexorable and dangerous purpose, as if there were no power in the universe that could stop it. All my life, everything important that had ever happened had always happened somewhere else. But *Sputnik* was right there in front of my eyes in my backyard in Coalwood, McDowell County, West Virginia, U.S.A. I couldn't believe it. I felt that if I stretched out enough, I could touch it. Then, in less than a minute, it was gone. . . . I kept closing my mouth and it kept falling open again. I had never seen anything so marvelous in my life. . . . I didn't want to break the spell *Sputnik* had cast over me. . . . That night, in my room, I kept thinking about *Sputnik* until I couldn't think about it anymore and fell asleep."[26]

The power of imagination to haunt and thus fuel passion is incredible. And the power of passion to haunt our imagination and frame our worldview is just as incredible. Reality consists mostly of what we can't see.[27] How we imagine unseen reality determines how we relate to what we can see. David had a God-dominated imagination. His only desire was that the whole world would know that there was a God in Israel.

Today we all find ourselves with the need to acquire a God-dominated imagination and to reject a Goliath-filled one.[28] That's what passion for God comes down to—imagination, our sense of reality. It's the only way we carry a giant's head—God has become so big in our thinking that everything else pales in insignificance.

I don't know what your particular intimidating giant is today. It may relate to your job, your spouse, or one of your children. Maybe it's a person, a lawsuit, unemployment, a health condition, some overwhelming temptation or habit. Financial worries, pornography, or how someone has hurt you deeply may dominate your thoughts. Or perhaps you can't get a handle on what that giant is. But it's there, haunting you. Uncertainty itself can be a giant. Whatever it is, God invites you right now to open your vision to Him.

Fill your imagination with God. Commute to where you can commune with God! Let your passion for God focus your sense of reality around Him. Take the time to pray, fill your heart with His Word, and meditate on His mighty acts and who He is—what He has already done for you and has promised yet to do. Practice His presence. Experience and rehearse His power already at work in your life. Take the initiative when giants appear. Keep the real issues crystal clear in your thinking. Determine to do a thorough work. Resolve now to trust Him fully. Finally, don't worry about coming to the end of your own strength. Remember how David put it? "The Lord does not deliver by sword or by spear; for the battle is the Lord's and He will give you into our hands" (1 Sam. 17:47, NASB). Say it the way David did: "The battle is Yours, Lord. It's Your battle. I lean on You. I give You all my weapons, all my skills, all my fears, this giant! And I stand before You, trusting You." Let your imagination be haunted by this kind of passion—God!

---

[1] Robert D. Bergen, *1, 2 Samuel,* pp. 196, 197.

[2] *Ibid.,* p. 195.

[3] *Ibid.,* pp. 197, 198.

[4] Warren W. Wiersbe, *Developing a Christian Imagination: An Interpretive Anthology* (Wheaton, Ill.: Victor Books, 1995), p. 9.

[5] Eugene Peterson, *Leap Over a Wall,* p. 39.

[6] "This passage presents the longest description of military attire in the Old Testament. Goliath's physical stature, armor, weaponry, and shield bearer must have made him appear invincible" (Bergen, p. 190).

[7] Ancient artwork depicted Philistine soldiers as wearing a feathered headdress, not a helmet. Goliath's headgear therefore was apparently atypical, designed for the special needs of representative or champion combat.

[8] Bergen, p. 189.

[9] *Ibid.,* p. 190.

[10] Peterson, p. 39.

[11] *Ibid.,* p. 40.

[12] *Ibid.*

[13] See Peterson, pp. 40-42.

[14] Theodore H. Epp, *A Man After the Heart of God*, p. 20.
[15] *Ibid.*, p. 21.
[16] *Ibid.*, p. 26.
[17] Bergen, p. 196.
[18] C. R. Swindoll, *David: A Man of Passion and Destiny*, p. 42.
[19] Epp, p. 23.
[20] Holmes Rolston, *Personalities Around David*, p. 26.
[21] *Ibid.*, p. 27.
[22] Ellen G. White, *Patriarchs and Prophets*, p. 645.
[23] Bergen, p. 196.
[24] Epp, p. 30.
[25] White, *Patriarchs and Prophets*, p. 452.
[26] Homer H. Hickam, Jr., *October Sky* (New York: Dell Publishing, 1999), pp. 38, 39.
[27] Peterson, p. 45.
[28] *Ibid.*, p. 39.

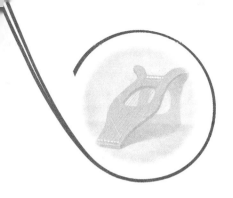

8

COMMON BONDS, UNCOMMON FRIENDS

1 Samuel 18:1-5

After his victory over Goliath, David's status rose to a lofty new level. It didn't take Saul long to have his military commander, Abner, call the young man in for an interview (1 Sam. 17:55-58). (I can see him there, standing before the king and Abner with Goliath's head in his hand.) Whenever Saul saw any mighty or valiant man, he attached him to his staff (1 Sam. 14:52). In fact, the king refused to let David return at all to his former life or work (1 Sam. 18:2).

One person in that crowd of astonished onlookers was Saul's oldest son, Jonathan, the crown prince. Scripture tells us that the young man found himself irresistibly drawn to David. "The soul of Jonathan was knit to the soul of David, and Jonathan loved him as himself" (verse 1, NASB). The Hebrew word translated *knit* literally means to tie or bind something to something else with a rope, a cord, or thread. Think about that—the soul of Jonathan tied to the soul of David. The Hebrew word for soul is *nephesh* and refers here to what one is deep down inside. It points to what people think and feel—their passion, emotions, values, priorities, and worldview. Jonathan and David are examples of two people bound together by something more powerful than circumstances and preferences. They were joined together at the deepest level of being, imagination, and passion.

As Jonathan stood in the wings watching David accept Goliath's challenge, and then saw him single-handedly slay the giant, his heart and mind flooded with memories of his own experience when God had delivered the Philistines into Israel's hands through him. Saul's son was no second-rate person. He was a man of ability in his own right—skilled with the bow, capable of facing down his violent father, unafraid to inspire his armor-bearer to follow him in attacking a Philistine garrison alone. A few years before, while commanding a thousand-plus men, he broke the Philistine morale and led his forces to victory (1 Sam. 14:13-15). His words of faith to his armor bearer are unforgettable —"Come and let us cross over to the garrison of these uncircumcised; perhaps the Lord will work for us, for the Lord is not restrained to save by many or by few" (verse 6, NASB). Just the two of them routed the garrison. As a result of his successes and personality, Jonathan enjoyed even greater popularity than his father.[1]

It is not surprising, then, that he immediately identified with David's experience of passion for the honor of God and victory over Goliath. He felt his soul strangely drawn to the God-honoring fellow Israelite. They had some important things in common. Both were courageous and capable warriors who possessed profound faith in the Lord. Both had initiated faith-motivated attacks against militarily superior Philistines that had resulted in great victories for Israel.[2] Both were men with hearts in tune with God. Both knew the Lord personally and understood His greatness.[3] Both had a passion for God's work and will. And both knew beyond a shadow of a doubt that they were fighting the Lord's battle—not their own.

Maybe David had beaten Jonathan to the draw, accomplishing what the king's son had been wishing to do all along—and done it without armor, shield, or sword. Perhaps Jonathan had hesitated to take on Goliath because he knew that ever since the Lord had departed from his father, all his father's weapons of defense failed him, that his people only reluctantly followed him (and then with trembling), and that Samuel had told him that his kingdom would not continue. I'm sure that Jonathan stayed with his father as if he hoped that by his own allegiance to God he might reverse the effects of Saul's failure. But as his father drifted further from God Jonathan's passion for God seemed to be of no avail. What could the son do to reverse the king's self-destructive decisions? Many a time as he heard the terrible roar of Goliath's challenge he must have felt the stirrings of a noble impulse to go out and meet him. To carry his head away as David finally had.[4] But he was paralyzed. Still, Jonathan recognized in David something of himself. They were like-minded Hebrew brothers who had a very clear understanding of God and were passionately committed to His cause.

David's faith and passion for God impressed Jonathan. Twice Scripture tells us that the king's son loved David as he did himself (1 Sam. 18:1, 3). Though Jonathan initiated the friendship, David quickly responded with deep love and commitment. Years later when his beloved friend died in battle David would lament, "I am distressed for you, my brother Jonathan; you have been very pleasant to me. Your love to me was more wonderful than the love of women" (2 Sam. 1:26, NASB). David and Jonathan were bound together in an inseparable relationship in which their minds and hearts became one. They were "soul brothers."

Passion sparks passion. That passion that responds to the passion of someone else can be either positive or negative, resonate or dissonant. It can be either stimulating or intimidating. Eliab considered David's passion for God intimidating, while Jonathan found it inspiring. David's passion for God stirred Eliab's heart to push his younger brother away in anger, but it drew Jonathan to David. Our passion for God can spark passion for Him in someone else's life or it can cause them to cry fanaticism or dig in their heels. We hear countless stories of people of passion sparking faith in someone else's life or eliciting an answering chord of faith from someone whose heart resonates with the same vision and passion for God.

I believe David's passion for God resulted from a sense of God's own passion. David saw God's passion expressed in His lovingkindness, His jealousy, His wrath against sin, His forgiveness, His judgments, and His mercy. Jürgen Moltmann observes how both the Old and New Testaments reveal the passion of God's heart. God displays great passion for creation, for human beings, and for the future. He who lives in a covenant relationship with this passionate God cannot remain apathetic.[5] Philip Yancey hints how God's favorites respond to His passion with passion in kind.[6] I believe that David sensed God's passion for him personally. And I also believe that David's passion for God stirred God Himself! Can you think of any better reason why God would say, "This guy is a man after My own heart. At the deepest level of our being, we resonate. He understands who I really am."

Those who respond to our passion for God often become very important people in our lives—even our best friends. And because they share our passion we stir one another up and inspire one another to better and more faithful service to God.[7] Together we have a common affection, vision, and bond. It knits hearts at the deepest level of being and imagination. That is what David and Jonathan experienced.

Passion sparks passion to even greater levels. Never forget that your passion for God can trigger passion in someone else's life. In return, let someone else's passion for God draw you toward similar passion for the Lord.

A Friend—No Matter What

Beyond this portrait of David and Jonathan's shared passion for God we catch a glimpse of what true passion-evoked friendship is all about. The biblical narrative focuses mainly on Jonathan, as David is the primary recipient in this friendship. According to this episode in David's story, true passion-inspired friendship has certain unique characteristics:

First, Scripture says that "Jonathan made a covenant with David because he loved him as himself" (1 Sam. 18:3, NIV). The word "covenant" in 1 Samuel 18:3 comes from the Hebrew *berith,* which points to a contractual agreement involving promises made between contracting parties and the establishment of guarantees or pledges. A covenant could be a treaty, an alliance of friendship, a pledge, an obligation between a monarch and his subjects, or a constitution. It was a personal contract accompanied by a sacrifice or solemn oath that sealed the relationship with promises of blessings or curses. David and Jonathan became soul brothers with a lifetime covenant. They vowed to be true and loyal friends the rest of their lives. All true relationships have their basis in some kind of bond or understanding—whether spoken or not. Promises and promises kept become a hallmark of identity, integrity, and intimacy.[8] Covenants stand behind any meaningful relationship.

Second, Jonathan honored David above himself. Because he was a prince and David a subject, Jonathan took the initiative. To the surprise of everyone, he sealed this contract with an act of kindness that some parts of the world still consider as the most significant honor one human being can bestow on another. As a prince, Jonathan clothed David with his own royal garments.[9] He stripped himself of his princely robe and gave it to David, along with his armor, including his sword, his bow, and his belt (verse 4). Jonathan wanted to give David something that belonged to him and was meaningful to him—something that pointed to his status and sense of identity. To honor another person above yourself when you are social equals is one thing, but to do so in Jonathan's situation is yet another. Here was the son of a king honoring a son of a shepherd! "Jonathan was well aware of the implications of what he was doing. He was heir to the throne of Israel, but with this act of humility, he was willing to step aside to make way for his *friend*. He truly believed David could do the job better than he could."[10] In David, Jonathan saw character fit for a king. He was so determined that the throne be occupied by God's chosen instrument that he offered everything he had. Jonathan was willing to sacrifice himself—for God's sake and for David's. His act symbolized that David would be king instead of him, something that Jonathan verified later when he said to David, "You will be king over Israel and I will be next to you" (1 Sam. 23:17, NASB).

That's the heart of a true friend. Individuals like Jonathan are a rarity. Few people will place the honor of others or the work of God ahead of their own favor and position. But that's what shared passion for God does. John the Baptist did it for Jesus when he said, "He must increase, but I must decrease" (John 3:30, NASB). Do you know anyone who has given up power or position for God's will? Someone who stepped aside for another who could do a better job?

Third, Jonathan was David's loyal defense when others would put David down and scheme behind his back. Not a fair-weather friend, he wouldn't talk against David when he wasn't around. Nor was he two-faced, being one way with David and another way with his father. "Jonathan spoke well of David to Saul his father" (1 Sam. 19:4, NIV). In fact, Saul's son not only defended his friend; he also rebuked his father for his negative attitude toward David: "Then Jonathan spoke well of David to Saul his father and said to him, 'Do not let the king sin against his servant David, since he has not sinned against you, and since his deeds have been very beneficial to you. For he took his life in his hand and struck the Philistine, and the Lord brought about a great deliverance for all Israel; you saw it and rejoiced. Why then will you sin against innocent blood by putting David to death without a cause?'" (verses 4, 5, NASB). We see here no pettiness, envy, jealousy, two-facedness, or hypocrisy—just loyalty.

Fourth, Jonathan remained David's authentic friend—no matter how difficult that kind of commitment eventually became. He lived out his covenantal friendship in circumstances that were markedly anti-David. "Friendship with David complicated Jonathan's life enormously. He risked losing his father's favor and willingly sacrificed his own royal future."[11] They were, as Beth Moore writes, "uncommon friends."[12] But neither the risk nor the loss deterred Jonathan's passionate loyalty. He stayed David's friend to the very end, living out his covenant during hard circumstances. Their covenant bond served God's purposes for David, but Jonathan got little out of it.[13] Many friendships similarly live out an existence in "Saul's court" as it were—in marital, family, work, and cultural conditions hostile to any vowed intimacy. But it's the covenant, not the conditions, that carries the day.[14] It's not what we get out of it, it's what it means to be a friend no matter the consequences. Only a shared passion for God and His plan or work can forge this kind of loyalty.

Fifth, Jonathan gave David a place to share his hurt without shame. Scripture records how when it became clear that David really did need to run for his life, he and Jonathan met in a field to say goodbye. His heart broke when Jonathan told him how his father had indeed determined to kill David and that they must part. David came out from where he had been hiding near a stone pile. As he did he fell on his face on the ground and bowed to Jonathan three times. Both of them were in tears as they embraced each other and said goodbye, but David wept the most (1 Sam. 20:41). They both knew how the recent turn of events meant separation. Jonathan had no choice but to be loyal to his father, and David would certainly have had it no other way. Though they would see very little of each other from that moment onward, they determined to never be separated in their hearts. "At last Jonathan said to David, 'Go in peace, for we have made a pact in the Lord's name. We have entrusted each other and each other's children into the Lord's hands forever'" (verse 42, NLT).

True friends are friends forever. Swindoll makes an interesting observation here: "When you've got a friend this close, knitted to your own soul, you don't have to explain why you do what you do. You just do it. . . . When your heart is broken, you can bleed all over a friend like this and he will understand. He won't confront you in your misery or share with you three verses, then tell you to straighten up. When a good friend is hurting, let him hurt. If a good friend feels like weeping, let him weep. If a good friend needs to complain, listen. An intimate friend doesn't bale; he's right there with you. You can be yourself, no matter what that self looks like."[15]

Beth Moore points to the link between such vulnerable sharing and one's passion for God: "Something about two men unafraid to share their hearts with one another never fails to move me. Uncommon friends can be vulnerable with one another and still retain their dignity. The friendship between Jonathan and David was far more than emotion, and it was a safe place to trust and show feelings. They shared a common goal: the will of God."[16]

Finally, Jonathan was a never-failing source of encouragement to David. Later we read how David received the news that Saul was on the way to Ziph to search for him and kill him. Jonathan went to find David and encouraged him to stay strong in his faith in God. "Don't be afraid," Jonathan reassured him. "My father will never find you! You are going to be the king of Israel, and I will be next to you, as my father is well aware" (see 1 Sam. 23:15-17). The unexpected visit came during a particularly discouraging time and brought a lot of joy to David. The moments they spent together in this wilderness refuge were precious. They related their varied experiences, and Jonathan strengthened the heart of David with those words of assurance that he would be Israel's next king and that he, Jonathan, would be right there supporting him. Ellen White tells us that "as they talked of the wonderful dealings of God with David, the hunted fugitive was greatly encouraged. . . . After the visit of Jonathan, David encouraged his soul with songs of praise, accompanying his voice with his harp."[17] Eugene Peterson suggests that Jonathan's friendship with David bracketed Saul's repeated attempts to kill David.[18] The friendship set boundaries to Saul's evil. Friends are a constant source of encouragement.

One of the Best Gifts

One of the most surprising facts about this story is the age disparity between Jonathan and David. David was about 20 or so when he killed

Goliath, while Jonathan was in his 30s or 40s and Saul somewhere in his 50s or 60s.[19] Scripture also tells that, years earlier, during the battle of Michmash, Saul had an adult son, Jonathan, who was a capable and seasoned warrior.[20] In other words, Jonathan was old enough to be David's father! When we keep in mind David's and Jonathan's respective ages we can understand their relationship more fully.[21]

Jonathan was one of the best gifts God ever gave to David.[22] It is highly unlikely that David could have persisted very long in either serving Saul or eluding him without Jonathan's friendship.[23] Ellen White asserts that the friendship of Jonathan for David was part of God's providence to preserve the life of Israel's future ruler.[24] The Lord would never have chosen David to be Israel's next king if He had not planned to sustain him and ultimately deliver him safely to the throne. Thus Jonathan was an important part of God's plan for him. God knew David needed an intimate friend to walk with him through the uneasy valley of the fugitive years that lay ahead.[25] Intimate friends are rare in life, and they can make the difference in whether we make it or not.[26] Jonathan's friendship with David was essential to the latter's life—both physically and emotionally. "Jonathan was one of the few positive things David had to fortify himself for the decade of fugitive living that lay just ahead."[27]

Ellen White writes: "Jonathan, by birth heir to the throne, yet knowing himself set aside by the divine decree; to his rival the most tender and faithful of friends, shielding David's life at the peril of his own; steadfast at his father's side through the dark days of his declining power, and at his side falling at the last—the name of Jonathan is treasured in heaven, and it stands on earth a witness to the existence and the power of unselfish love."[28] It's a great thing to *have* a Jonathan. And it's a great thing to *be* a Jonathan.

Paul received an automobile from his brother as a Christmas present. On Christmas Eve when he left his office, a street urchin was walking around the shiny new car, admiring it. "Is this your car, mister?" he asked.

Paul nodded. "My brother gave it to me for Christmas."

The boy was astounded. "You mean your brother gave it to you and it didn't cost you nothing? Boy, I wish . . ." He hesitated. Of course Paul knew what he was going to wish for—that he had a brother like that. But what the lad said jarred Paul all the way down to his heels. "I wish," the boy went on, "that I could be a brother like that."[29]

When I think of Jonathan, I cannot help saying to myself, "I wish I were a brother like that!" How about you? And to whom should you be such a brother—or sister?

God wants you to do what Jonathan did. Let your heart be drawn out toward someone who has an authentic passion for God, then share that passion for Him and His work to a dying world. Allow God to use you to encourage and protect that passion in someone else. Remember: "Friendship *forms.*"[30] It not only can make a difference in the vitality of your own passion for God, it can strengthen someone else's passion for God as well.

When I think how David's passion for God drew Jonathan to join him in such a deeply personal way, I remember my friend Stuart Peters. Stu lived grandly in every arena of his life. And when he gave his life to Jesus, he lived large for God as well. He had a faith-based optimism, a "give-me-this-mountain" kind of attitude, and a commanding presence that quickly captured my heart. His size, his imagination, his originality, his attitude, his enthusiasm for whatever was at hand, his generosity, his investment in life, and his love for God seized everyone within his reach. He was the polestar around which everyone took their bearings.

My friend was clearly in charge of his world, and everyone knew it. Even his grandkids affectionately called him Stu, not Grandpa or Pap Pap, with a careful mix of reverence and a bit of his cockiness. He was a successful entrepreneur who dreamed big, worked hard, demanded the best of those around him, drove big cars, loved to eat out, and always carried $100 bills folded in his pocket. But Stu also had a soft heart of gratefulness to God and the gentle spirit of a servant. And he loved his family dearly. No one was more important to him than his family.

When I first met Stu I was fresh out of seminary on my first assignment and 25 years old. Stu was fresh out of the baptistry—and old enough to be my dad. I was a pastor. He was a business entrepreneur. The strength of his passion for Jesus drew me into his world. We became fast friends who shared a vision for God. For seven years we worked together building up that small church into a thriving Adventist congregation.

Responding to such passion, I found myself quickly drawn into Stu's large world and loved like family. But he was more than a dad to me. Stu was my best friend, the closest I've ever known. We would hang out at his favorite restaurant to talk about life and shared a yearly pilgrimage to Easton, Maryland's, waterfowl festival. Dreaming of how we might start a new ministry, we gave Bible studies together, visited discouraged members, and prayed for people in need. Many times I heard Stu pray for a "strong angel" to come by my side, or to be present in a situation someone was facing. More than once I witnessed the eyes of this man-in-charge-of-life fill with tears over someone's need, or over someone's victory. His care for others was practical as much as it was emotional. Stu's generosity blessed everyone within his reach and built up God's church far beyond.

The most vivid memories, though, were packed into the 21 days we spent touring the Middle East just before I was scheduled to move from the small church family we'd invested so much in. Surrounded by a busload of fellow tourists we had never met until we got on the plane together, I watched him nurture and encourage and befriend. I found myself involved in a continual conversation of spiritual lessons as we took in the sights and history and meaning of the Bible lands—from Jordan to Israel to Egypt to Greece. I joined him in his gravelly rendition of that melancholy chorus, "El Shaddai, El Shaddai, . . . I will love You 'til I die." As I look back I realize it was a poignant capstone to God's work in his life. A few months later doctors diagnosed Stu as having a rare brain cancer. He endured a few intense weeks of suffering and faith, then I found myself standing at his casket, singing the same strains. Stu's voice had been silenced, but his passion had not ended. Because, as I had watched this man of God grow, I responded with a longing to grow myself.

Stu was one of those "very important people" we've been learning about. He inspired and touched me in a deeply personal way. But all along I realized I figured large in Stu's heart too. Although he was old enough to be my dad, I know he looked to me to find inspiration to live larger for God. Something about my passion for God in turn sparked his. I know he drew on my spiritual resources to enlarge his own. Ours was an uncommon friendship sharing a common goal: the will of God.

Stu is resting, waiting for his "strong angel" to awaken him, but each fall as the Canada geese call overhead and remind me of him, my soul pleads for God to let me live the passion that Stu stirred in me. Let me live it until Jesus comes, when together once again we can sing of our love for

El Shaddai.

Passion sparks passion and is stirred by passion. It gets passed on to become greater passion. And what God accomplishes in one life multiplies a thousandfold by the fire it ignites in others.

[1] His popularity caused the people to reject Saul's foolish leadership and protect him against his father's thoughtless decree. See 1 Samuel 14:44, 45.

[2] Robert D. Bergen, *1, 2 Samuel*, p. 199.

[3] Gene A. Getz, *David: Seeking God Faithfully*, p. 78.

[4] F. B. Meyer, *The Life of David*, p. 49.

[5] Jürgen Moltmann, "The Passion of Life," *Currents in Theology and Mission* 4, no. 1 (February 1977): 6, 7.

[6] Philip Yancey, *Reaching for the Invisible God*, pp. 188-192.

[7] Gordon MacDonald, *Restoring Your Spiritual Passion*, pp. 76-78.

[8] David F. Wells, *Losing Our Virtue: Why the Church Must Recover Its Moral Vision* (Grand Rapids: William B. Eerdmans Publishing Co., 1998), pp. 144, 145.

[9] Getz, p. 63.

[10] *Ibid.*, p. 79.

[11] Eugene Peterson, *Leap Over a Wall*, p. 53.

[12] Beth Moore, *A Heart Like His: Intimate Reflections on the Life of David* (Nashville: Broadman and Holman Publishers, 1999), p. 68.

[13] Peterson, p. 53.

[14] *Ibid.*, p. 54.

[15] Charles R. Swindoll, *David: A Man of Passion and Destiny*, p. 54.

[16] Moore, p. 70.

[17] Ellen G. White, *My Life Today* (Washington, D.C.: Review and Herald Pub. Assn., 1952), p. 210.

[18] Peterson, pp. 52, 53.

[19] First Samuel 13:1 (NASB) tells us that Saul was 40 years old when he began to reign, and he reigned 32 years over Israel. At the time Jonathan was commanding 1,000 men, which means he was at least 20 years old.

[20] Alden Thompson, *The Abundant Bible Amplifier: Samuel*, ed. George R. Knight (Boise, Idaho: Pacific Press Pub. Assn., 1995), p. 103.

[21] Keith Kaynor, *When God Chooses*, pp. 52-55.

[22] *Ibid.*, p. 52.

[23] Peterson, p. 53.

[24] White, *My Life Today*, p. 210.

[25] Moore, p. 68.

[26] Swindoll, p. 52.

[27] Kaynor, p. 53.

[28] White, *Education*, p. 157.

[29] Dan Clark, "A Brother Like That," *Chicken Soup for the Soul: 101 Stories to Open the Heart and Rekindle the Spirit*, ed. Jack Canfield and Mark Victor Hansen (Deerfield Beach, Fla.: Health Communications, Inc., 1993), pp. 25, 26.

[30] Peterson, p. 53.

9

THE SACRED ROMANCE

Psalm 18:1

So far, what have we learned? First, that passion *claims it all*—one's whole being. It is what the heart seeks, but it demands the whole heart—all the heart and soul and strength and mind. Everything or nothing. Only when passion claims the whole heart can we say that it has truly seized *us* rather than our trying to create it or fake it.

Second, passion *yields it all*. It not only *claims it all*; it presses the heart to *yield it all* as well. You cannot have passion if you are not willing to give yourself fully to the goal of that passion.

Third, passion *is imaginative*. It fills the heart with art. Nothing remains status quo or colorless. Rather, it produces inspiration that leads to creativity and freshness. When passion *claims it all* and *yields it all* for some compelling cause or experience or object or being or relationship, an imaginativeness frames everything we do.

Fourth, passion *constantly renews itself*. Yesterday's passion cannot provide today's inner energy. Passion quickly dissipates and must be restored regularly. By nature passion gravitates toward whatever inspires it, thirsting for more of it—thus renewing itself. Living by your passion keeps your passion stirred.

Fifth, passion *hears what it wants to hear*. It has selective hearing, choosing who or what it listens to. It will not open itself indiscriminately to just any voice or influence that might sidetrack its vision, focus, or vitality.

Sixth, passion *has purpose, a reason for being, an agenda*—something that it is willing to spend and be spent for. Without a purpose or reason for being, passion is either impossible or empty—mere emotionalism, zeal without knowledge, lacking real meaning or direction.

Seventh, passion *haunts the imagination*—our worldview. Whatever vision of reality dominates our inner private world will become our passion. Once passion for something awakens, it can so dominate our perception of reality that our imagination will be both imprinted with and centered around that very vision.

Eighth, passion *evokes passion*. Your passion for some cause or some person can spark a similar passion in another individual's life. That responding passion can be either positive or negative, stimulating or intimidating. We can turn people on or off, drawing them to us or driving them away from both us as people and whatever is important to us.

Each one of these facets of passion revolves around one inescapable reality—passion is deeply personal. It is experienced and expressed by a personal being—you, me, or God. Furthermore, passion is personal because it is experienced and expressed most powerfully and most perfectly when directed toward another personal being.

Because passion deals largely with the heart it involves the meaning of our lives and the purpose of our existence. It expresses who we are deep inside—our values, our choices, our sense of reality, our creativity, what captures our imagination, what we're willing to commit ourselves to, and what we truly love. Passion also reveals the affective level on which we live our life—personal or impersonal, intimate or emotionally detached, I-thou or I-it. Our passion for a hobby, an object, a compelling cause, a project, an ideology, or a religious experience can be intensely personal because we are caught up in it. The experience of passion consumes *our* time and *our* energy and *our* resources and *our* creative juices. Furthermore, passion feels. Never a matter of cold, heartless, calculating logic or energy, it brings to the forefront our emotions as we experience and express our passion (though passion is not emotionalism). Thus we can find our purpose for existence and the meaning of life (and quite a lot of feeling) in *things* and *ideas* and *causes*. While on the one hand all this is intensely personal because *we* are the ones experiencing and expressing and feeling this passion as personal beings, on the other hand, in reality, such passion is itself impersonal (and thus dispassionate) because the very things and ideas and causes that stir *our* passion are themselves impersonal—mere objects or ideas. While passion genuinely *feels* on this impersonal level, it does not have the same depth or power or genuineness as when it opens itself to another personal being.

The intimacy involved in person-to-person relationships is what makes passion whole and truly personal. Likewise, the intimacy of person-to-person passion defines us most clearly. Again, passion reveals the affective level on which we live our life—personal or impersonal, intimate or emotionally detached, I-thou or I-it. What will it be? When we avoid intimacy our heart never fully engages itself with whatever we are passionate toward. But when we pursue intimacy we are involved on the deepest level of our being and our passion expresses that greater reality. Intimacy implies love, affection, closeness, transparency, commitment, and self-surrender. While we can have passion for things and ideas and causes, we cannot truly *love* them. Nor can we have affection for an idea or be emotionally close to a thing. Above all, it is impossible to be transparent before a cause. Such transparency can be experienced only before the gaze of an intelligent and moral other. We might be committed to a cause or an idea and surrender ourself to it, but it's not the same as giving ourselves to a person or making a commitment to someone. Only on the person-to-person level is passion at its best. Passion is personal and leads to intimacy. But intimacy itself generates passion as well.[1] It's a simple equation. No passion, no intimacy. No intimacy, no passion. Thus intimacy makes life a passion.

I Love You, God—

The single most characteristic thing about David was his relationship to God. David opened his heart to God, loved God, believed God, thought about God, imagined God, addressed God, prayed to God, sang to God, obeyed God—in other words, framed his whole world with God. The largest part of David's existence wasn't himself or things or theology or a worthwhile cause, but God. He felt more passionately about God than about anything else in the world.[2] His strongest instinct was to relate his life to God. In comparison, nothing else really mattered.[3] This is what attracts us to David, not his vigor or his energy or that everything he did was done with consummate passion. It's his intimacy with God that haunts us—the person-to-person passion.

To David, God was alive—a living, personal being. The Lord was someone he knew and spoke to. At the same time, God loved and cared for him, both commanding and protecting him. He was close by and involved in both David's life and the world at large. And God Himself was deeply passionate. He awakened intimate passion on the personal level. David sensed both God's immediacy and His passion for him personally. Because God was personal and present, He required a personal *response*. Again, David's psalms reveal the inner reality of his heart and passion. They abound with intimate imagery and the personal and a recognition that God could be hurt in their relationship:

"I love you, Lord;
>you are my strength" (Ps. 18:1, NLT).

"I will be filled with joy because of you.
>I will sing praises to your name, O Most High" (Ps. 9:2, NLT).

"Listen to my cry for help, my King and my God,
>for to you I pray" (Ps. 5:2, NIV).

"I said to the Lord, 'You are my Lord;
>apart from you I have no good thing'" (Ps. 16:2, NIV).

"You will make known to me the path of life;
>In Your presence is fullness of joy;
>In Your right hand there are pleasures forever" (Ps. 16:11, NASB).

"O God, you are my God, earnestly I seek you;
>my soul thirsts for you, my body longs for you,
>in a dry and weary land where there is no water. . . .

"Because your love is better than life,
>my lips will glorify you.

"I will praise you as long as I live,
>and in your name I will lift up my hands. . . .

"On my bed I remember you;
>I think of you through the watches of the night. . . .

"My soul clings to you;
>your right hand upholds me" (Ps. 63:1-8, NIV).

"I will give thanks to You, O Lord my God, with all my heart,
   and will glorify Your name forever" (Ps. 86:12, NASB).
"I will sing of lovingkindness and justice,
   to You, O Lord, I will sing praises" (Ps. 101:1, NASB).
"To You, O Lord, I lift up my soul" (Ps. 25:1, NKJV).
"When You said, 'Seek My face,'
   my heart said to You, 'Your face, O Lord, I shall seek'"
                                                    (Ps. 27:8, NASB).
"I will love You . . . I will run for dear life to You . . . I cry for help to
You . . . I will sing to You . . . I lift up my soul to You . . . I will give thanks
to You . . . I will seek Your face . . . My soul clings to You . . . I find all
my good in You." These excerpts depict an extraordinarily wide range of
personal response. But they all share personal immediacy. God required a
personal response, and He got it from David. It's hard for me to read these
deeply personal expressions of passion for God without reflecting on how
I personally relate to God. Is my God absent, distant, or impersonal? Or
is He present, close, and personal? Do I know *about* God, or do I *know*
God? Do I believe *in* God, or do I *believe* God?

The stories from David's youthful years provide vivid imagery of the
personal nature of his passion for God. Whether it haunted his imagination or focused his creative energy or compelled him with purpose,
David's passion was for God. Three moments in David's later life further
highlight the deeply personal nature of his passion for God. Following his
adulterous affair with Bathsheba and the murder of her husband, Uriah,
we find Israel's king lying prostrate on the ground for six straight nights
in anguished contrition and tearfully writing an open psalm of personal
confession to be sung throughout the land and ultimately around the
world—a psalm exposing the true nature of sin as intensely personal and
involving a broken relationship with God (Ps. 51): "Have mercy on me, O
God, because of your unfailing love. Because of your great compassion,
blot out the stain of my sins. Wash me clean from my guilt. Purify me
from my sin. For I recognize my shameful deeds—they haunt me day and
night. Against you, and you alone, have I sinned; I have done what is evil
in your sight. You will be proved right in what you say, and your judgment against me is just" (verses 1-4, NLT). David both sinned and confessed before a one-Person audience. Both sin and confession are

interpersonal realities. They imply intimacy (or its lack) and convey the personal quality of passion.

Later, when David aspired to build God a house that would be better than his own royal palace, God said, "No! You won't build Me a house. Rather, I will build you a house. I will make you great in character, reputation, material blessings, and lineage. Your house and your kingdom will endure forever before Me; your throne will be established forever" (see 2 Sam. 7:5-17). So, in the midst of dreaming big things for God, David realizes that the Lord has something even bigger in mind for him. He is overwhelmed by grace and awestruck with humility. We find him quietly entering the sacred tent that housed the ark and sitting down (verse 18). I imagine a long period of silence as he just sat there. David had a lot on his mind, a lot to think about. Finally, he offers a prayer full of God and ends with some soul-haunting questions: "Who am I, O Sovereign Lord, and what is my family, that you have brought me this far? And now, Sovereign Lord, in addition to everything else, you speak of giving me a lasting dynasty! Do you deal with everyone this way, O Sovereign Lord? What more can I say? You know what I am really like, Sovereign Lord. For the sake of your promise and according to your will, you have done all these great things and have shown them to me'" (verses 18-21, NLT).

One of the most beautifully reverent passages in all the Bible, it tenderly portrays an affectionate relationship between God and one of His children. It provides an intimate glimpse into David's very heart and mind. We receive a private view of his attitude toward God. David knew what it was like to have intimate communion with God. "Who am I, O Sovereign Lord, and what is my family, that you have brought me this far?" he asks (verse 18, NLT). "Are you like this with everyone?" "Do you deal with everyone this way?" he wonders out loud (verse 19, NLT). "You know all about me." "You know what I am really like," he confesses (verse 20, NLT). Talk about intimacy! This is person-to-person passion. David to God. God to David. And David back to God.

Keenly aware of God's capacity to explore the human heart, he prayed, "You have searched me and you know me" (Ps. 139:1, NIV). David does not reveal when or under what circumstances he was compelled to write about this particular moment of divine probing, but it was diligent, difficult, and intensely personal. *"You* have searched *me!"* he writes. "You are exploring and digging into me through and through, searching for telling facts and information for building a picture of my character—who I really am deep down inside. My most common and casual moments are completely familiar to You. Even my thoughts are an open book in Your hand. In fact, You monitor the whole process of my thought-life. You see and understand what goes on inside me, knowing what makes me tick and why I am who I am, and do what I do" (see verses 1-6). "This blows my mind," David finally cries (see verse 6). It's hard to believe. In fact, it's scary. It makes me want to run and hide. To flee from Your face. But "where can I go from your Spirit? Where can I flee from your presence? If I go up to the heavens, you are there; if I make my bed in the depths, you are there. If I rise on the wings of the dawn, if I settle on the far side of the sea, even there your hand will guide me, your right hand will hold me fast. If I say, 'Surely the darkness will hide me and the light become night around me,' even the darkness will not be dark to you; the night will shine like the day, for darkness is as light to you" (verses 7-12, NIV).

The things God knew about him could have made David nervous, yet he prays, "Search me, O God, and know my heart; try me and know my anxious thoughts; and see if there be any hurtful way in me, and lead me in the everlasting way" (verses 23, 24, NASB). He is not afraid of intimacy at its most basic level—transparency before the eyes of a morally intelligent other. David wants to be God's man at any cost, so he unveils his inner being, purposefully, consciously, down where unspoken thoughts dwell and unstated motives hide out in secret. Not only does he invite God's searchlight, David goes even further. He asks the Lord to find out which thoughts or tendencies lead him away from fellowship with God. "Show them to me so I can understand them and their effect on my walk with You," he says. That's intimacy. And that's passion! Only open, transparent hearts can be seized by authentic passion. The kind of intimacy and openness this psalm implies generates passion—a desire to be real, and close. No openness, no intimacy, no passion. If we don't allow God to get close enough to really know what we're like (even though He already does), we'll never get close enough to Him to find out what He's really like.

Susie attended the evening baptismal class I was teaching for an evangelist who was holding public lectures where I pastored. Early on, this petite young woman in her late 20s had confided to me that she had divorced an abusive husband and had recently moved out of a live-in relationship with another guy who was encouraging her to be a stripper and pose for pornographic media. During one evening's discussion on some of the basics of the Christian life, she raised her hand and asked, "Do I have to name my sins when I confess, or can I just ask God to forgive my sins, period? I mean, do I have to get specific?"

We discussed the merits of an itemized list versus blanket coverage and talked about the difference between our being a sinner and committing specific sins (we sin because we are sinners, not vice versa). I suggested that we needed to express both in confession to God—the itemized list and the desire for blanket coverage—because we *are* sinners. Also, I observed that a foggy notion of sin creates a foggy understanding of our need for the atoning work of Jesus. The more specific and concrete we are in confession, the more likely that we will recognize we are sinners in need of God's grace. And the work of Jesus on our behalf will appear more desirable. As was the case with the woman who anointed the feet of Jesus—she loved much because she was forgiven much, as opposed to those who love little because they have been forgiven little (Luke 7:47). Passion for God is obviously proportionate to our sense of who we are and how much Jesus has redeemed us.

Following the class that night Susie pulled me aside and whispered, "I am so ashamed to tell God what I've done. It's so intimate. Doesn't He already know?"

"Susie," I said, "tell God all that personal stuff as if He'd never heard it before, because in the very process, you will be opening yourself to Him as you never have before. That's how your heart will melt before Him in total surrender and you will cling to Him as your only hope. The work of Jesus will be so much more precious to you. Do it!"

The love, or affection, or closeness, or transparency, or self-surrender, or commitment of intimacy is deeply existential—reaching to the very core of who we are. It's not easy, but it's the stuff of real passion—being personal with God (and in the process, being truly personal within).

The Passion of My Own Heart

A sense of God's passion stirred passion in David's heart. He saw that divine passion both expressed in God's created works and mighty acts and as God extended it toward him personally. The passion of God's heart appears throughout Scripture but never more clearly and intimately than in the life of David and the imagery of his poetry and psalms. David knew by experience that one cannot live long in relationship with this passionate God and remain apathetic.[4] Those who respond to God's passion usually do so with their own passion. God's person and ways awaken intimacy, beckoning such passion on the personal level. I believe, too, that the intimacy of David's passion for God stirred God Himself! As I've asked in an earlier chapter (discussing how passion evokes passion), can you think of any better reason that God would say, "This guy is a man after My own heart. At the deepest level of our being, we resonate. He understands who I really am"? The relationship got to God as well.[5] He went out of His way both to make and to keep covenant promises with David. One finds in Scripture an incredible commitment on His part toward His friend David: "I have found David my servant; with my sacred oil I have anointed him. My hand will sustain him; surely my arm will strengthen him. . . . My faithful love will be with him. . . . I will maintain my love to him forever, and my covenant with him will never fail. I will establish his line forever, his throne as long as the heavens endure. . . . I will not take my love from him, nor will I ever betray my faithfulness. I will not violate my covenant or alter what my lips have uttered. Once for all, I have sworn by my holiness—and I will not lie to David" (Ps. 89:20-35, NIV). One can only wonder just what this relationship between David and God was like. The promise is that the intimacy of our own passion for God can get to Him too. He will do the same with you and me—make and keep incredible promises.

Only on the person-to-person level is passion for God really real, because genuine passion for God can only be personal. It leads to intimacy with God, and that very intimacy generates passion for Him as well. It's a simple equation. No passion for God, no intimacy with Him. No intimacy with God, no true passion for Him. When we pursue intimacy with God we are engaged on the deepest level of our being, and our passion for Him will express that deeper reality. Scripture repeatedly emphasizes a relationship with a Person rather than a doctrinal system, mystical experience, or spiritual technique.[6] What will it be? Things, causes, ideas—or God? Intimacy or emotional detachment? I-Thou or I-it? Intimacy with God implies love, affection, closeness, transparency, commitment, and self-surrender. Can you handle that? That's what I want. Passion. David's passion. Passion for God.

Do you know what you are passionate about? That's what I keep asking myself whenever I think very long about David—"What am I passionate about? And why? Am I a man of passion—with overwhelming passion for God? Do I have a heart like His? How intimate with Him have I become?"

David invites you to "open your mouth and taste, open your eyes and see—how good God is" (see Ps. 34:8).

---

[1] Gordon MacDonald, *Restoring Your Spiritual Passion,* p. 211.
[2] Philip Yancey, *Reaching for the Invisible God,* p. 190.
[3] *Ibid.,* p. 192.
[4] Jürgen Moltmann, "The Passion of Life," pp. 6, 7.
[5] Yancey, p. 192.
[6] *Ibid.,* p. 188.

Epilogue

YOUR STRONGEST INSTINCT

Stories from David's early years provide us vivid imagery of his passion for God. They focus on his initial fervor and wholeheartedness when God first became the absolute center of his everything. From his youth David was an authentic man of passion with an overwhelming passion for God. He felt more passionately about God than about anything else in the world, and during his later reign as Israel's king that message trickled down to the entire nation. It's no wonder that his people lost their heart to him more than to any other king, and that it would be David alone who figures large in its life, memory, and imagination. That message still lingers even after so many centuries.

David's youthful years captivate us because they are filled with so much innocence, energy, vigor, and simple faith. That's what I want, and I never want to lose it. This is why I keep thumbing back to the story of David. I know no better model for a passionate relationship with God. And this is why God wants me to know David. He wants me to know David because He wants me to have *a heart like his/His.* The shepherd-psalmist is the only recorded human being ever referred to by God Himself as having such a heart. When the Lord looked through the land in search of a new king for Israel, only David had the kind of heart whose strongest instinct was to relate its life to God. David early nurtured the heart qualities and disciplines that would both awaken and sustain passion for God.

A passion is necessary in my walk with God lest my spiritual life become crammed with events (not experience), contacts (not relationships), ideas (not soul), and things (not truthfulness). I shudder at the thought that I would ever come to the place where I "go through the motions"—performing out of habit more than anything else. Or that there would no longer be any energy to my faith experience, because I have allocated it toward something other than God (the pursuit of a career position, a hobby or recreational effort, or some activity that appears more daring, more pleasurable, or more personally affirming). Do God and faith and my Adventist hope still grab my imagination as they did in my younger years when I first believed? When Jesus comes, will He find spiritual passion still burning in me? My heart resists boredom or lukewarmness, and I never want to be lukewarm.

How about you? What is your heart like? What is your passion quotient? your strongest instinct? How would you answer the urgent questions that David's story raises about your heart? Does passion for God claim all your heart, leading you to yield your very all to Him? What about your creative juices? Does passion for God stir and channel them toward Him and His glory? Are you a commuter—incessantly renewing your passion for God by taking time to be with Him, hear His Word, and pray?

What purpose drives your soul? What cause calls you forth? Is it God? And does your passion for God make Him so dominant in your imagination that everything else pales in significance? What kind of response does your passion evoke in others? Is your passion for God intimate and personal? Do you know God or do you merely know about Him? Does the fire still burn since you first believed? Has it ever burned? Are you lukewarm or hot, halfhearted or wholehearted, passionless or passionate for God?

We identify easily with David—his temptations and struggles, and with the interwoven tangle of sin and obedience, success and failure, and drama and boredom that filled the days of his life. We all see bits of ourselves in his life. His temptations and failures are like our own. They warn us. His courage, faithfulness, and passion for God set an example for us to follow. Yet David's story yields more than mere biblical principles about life. It is more than a vivid example of passion and its varied facets—even passion for God. The story of David reveals God to us. More about God than David, it points us to what God is like and what He has done. Through this man David God is showing us something about Himself. David had a heart like His. What does this tell us about God? and passion? Why is God worthy of such a thing?

Some of the answers to these questions will be answered better in the next volumes on David's story, but his youthful years point to a God who looks into our hearts to see what we are really like deep down inside, who claims all our heart, who asks us to yield ourselves completely to Him in heartfelt obedience, and who beckons us toward intimacy with Himself, and would so dominate our imagination and compel us toward His glory that we are empowered to overcome any and every giant we would ever face. David's passion tells us that God, too, is passionate. The Lord's person and ways and Word awaken intimacy. They beckon my passion on the personal level. And the very intimacy of my passion for God can powerfully stir God Himself! It's incredible when you think about it. God is personal and so very near and real. He requires *response*—a personal response. Passion!